SHALEEA VENNEY, LVN

Little Girl, Little Girl, Don't Get Lost In This World

First published by Shaleea Venney 2019

Copyright © 2019 by Shaleea Venney, LVN

All rights reserved. No part of this publication may be reproduced, stored or transmitted in any form or by any means, electronic, mechanical, photocopying, recording, scanning, or otherwise without written permission from the publisher. It is illegal to copy this book, post it to a website, or distribute it by any other means without permission.

Shaleea Venney, LVN asserts the moral right to be identified as the author of this work.

Designations used by companies to distinguish their products are often claimed as trademarks. All brand names and product names used in this book and on its cover are trade names, service marks, trademarks and registered trademarks of their respective owners. The publishers and the book are not associated with any product or vendor mentioned in this book. None of the companies referenced within the book have endorsed the book.

First edition

This book was professionally typeset on Reedsy. Find out more at reedsy.com

*To my beautiful daughter Khaleea- I have loved you since the first time I felt you swish around in my belly. I had you when I was a baby myself. This is my gift to you. This is my heart and soul in paper form. I have been writing it quietly in my mind since you suddenly came into this world in 2004. I finally decided to write it down. If anything were to ever happen to me, you would have my love and guidance here in this book. Always trust God and pray, trust yourself, walk in love, and be confident in your abilities and you will go far. This is your book. I love you more than you will ever know-
Mom.*

Contents

Preface		iii
1	Fatherless Girls	1
2	Parents	5
3	Motherless Daughters	8
4	Self-Love/Your Perception	13
5	Periods: Toxic Shock Syndrome	17
6	The Boy/Don't Settle For the First Guy Who Looks At You	21
7	Cold Porcelain/Losing Your Virginity	25
8	Teenage Motherhood/Sex	31
9	Promiscuity	39
10	Love	44
11	Peer Pressure (The "In" Crowd)	51
12	Don't Be in Such A Rush To Grow Up/You Can't Get Your Youth...	56
13	Role Models/ What Are You Seeing?	60
14	Education	64
15	Set Future Goals	67
16	Depression	71
17	Bullying	75
18	Molestation	80
19	Don't Ever Get Too Big To Pray!	84
20	Give Yourself Some Credit (Cards!)	88
21	Closing Thoughts	94
22	Your Mistakes Are A Part of You, but Don't Define You	97

23	Might I Suggest You See The World?	100
24	I'm A Big Girl Now	103
25	Give Thanks!	109
About the Author		111

Preface

"When I grow up, I want to be a famous writer and lawyer!" If you'd have met the childhood version of me, this is what she would proudly proclaim to you if you would've asked. Nobody told that inexperienced little girl that there was the slightest chance that life would not happen as she had dreamed. There was never a notion that this would be a dream deferred. I lost my way and ended up completely on the other side of my dream. I had had a child, dropped out of school, and became a statistic at the age of 16. How did this happen? How did I go from getting acceptance letters from Universities and being on the honor roll as a straight A student, to getting acceptance letters for food stamps, and standing in the Welfare line?

Growing up today has to be the hardest time ever in the history of growing up as a girl. Everywhere you look, there's young ladies dressing sexier, acting sexier and growing up more quickly than the generation before it. The young ladies of today have so many more pressures than we had just 10-15 years ago. There's a huge emphasis on sex, and what it means to be "hot". When you listen to the songs on the radio, watch the music videos, or use social media one thing is for sure: Things have changed.

Even the "Good girl" can be tempted by popularity, peers, boys and advertisements. We live in a world where bad is good, good is boring, and where you can be famous for being famous. All you have to do is look good and you can be rich. Not born beautiful? Don't worry, you can buy any body part that you want. You could always marry a rich athlete or musician because women are here to be seen and not heard. Why stay in school and struggle to get the grade, when the girl next door is making it big because of an Instagram video she posted showing off her assets? Or a YouTube video that went "Viral"? What is the incentive to keep you on the straight and narrow in today's society?

The voice of the good little girl inside of you can quickly become a whisper when you make choices based off emotions rather than your mind and common sense. We all start out as ambitious little girls and then life happens. Life will happen to you too. There'll be times when you'll have to make a decision that could potentially impact your whole life in a matter of minutes. These bad decisions can cause you to lose yourself. You'll search high and low for years sometimes trying to find her again. So, what do you do? Life isn't going to stop and wait for you and you most definitely are not going to be immune to drama, trials, and heartache.

Might I make a suggestion? Little girl, little girl…don't get lost in this world.

1

Fatherless Girls

"We have no say on how we come into this world or the circumstances behind it. When we are born, we do not get to choose who we go home from the hospital with."
-Shaleea Venney

I once saw a quote that read: "A father is his daughters' first love and his sons' first hero". That quote has stuck with me through the years because of the truth behind it. So many young women are walking around with an emptiness and a longing for the love that their dad never shared.

Maybe you never met your father and were raised by your mother, grandparents, or other relatives. Maybe your parents are divorced, and he doesn't have time for you. Perhaps your father was there every day of your life, but you never felt like he was *really* "There".

Some of your fathers aren't very good people from a moral standpoint. They could be womanizers, convicts, or maybe you witnessed them beating on your mother's. It is possible that your father never keeps his word when he tells you he is going to do something.

You may be the result of a one-night stand or your father could be married to another woman and wants nothing to do with you. Your father might not even know you exist because he and your mother stopped speaking and she never told him she was with child. Maybe your parents have a great marriage and your father treats you like a princess.

No matter which of these scenarios you can identify with, it's NOT your fault. We have no say on how we come into this world or the circumstances behind it. When we are born, we do not get to choose who we go home from the hospital with.

The relationship you share with your father will greatly affect the rest of your life. If your father never tells you how beautiful you are to him, you will likely believe the first knucklehead who utters those words. If your father beat your mother, it is likely you will find a similar suitor when you begin to be in relationships because it is your normal. If your father doesn't act like he cherishes you, you may run in and out of many arms looking for that love and you will not find it. When your father constantly lies about the things he says he'll do, there's a good chance your spouse will too one day. Your fathers' dishonesty only teaches you to accept this kind of behavior. Your father is ultimately your role model and the standard for what a man should be.

Even if your father was not perfect or you never had a father at all, don't let the situation hinder you in life. The disconnection you had with him led to your first heartbreak. Forgive him. You need to forgive him and not hold his parenting skills or lack thereof, against him. He hopefully did what he thought was best and was acting from a place of love. You can't judge him. You don't know how his father treated him or if he is harboring some sort of pain from his own childhood that he hasn't yet come to terms with. Don't judge him. Love him just the same. When you learn to let go of what your ideal father should look like and love the one that you have for who he is and who he wants to be, you can significantly diminish your pain.

I'll be honest, letting go is not always easy. My father is probably the most selfish man in my life. He always has been. He's an only child and he grew up more spoiled than he'd admit today. My grandfather worked hard and made sure that his family was well taken care of. My father is very spoiled and entitled because of this. He never wanted to work hard for anything. His lack of motivation landed him in prison because he was always looking for a quick come up through some get rich quick scheme. He's lied and stolen to get by for most of his life. The saddest thing is he's smart. He plays the saxophone, and golf, and can read music. If only he'd applied himself, he could've been successful. I can literally remember about 6 Christmas' in a row that my father missed because he was in prison. I would write him letters often.

My father's biggest problem is that he has a sense of superiority. He looks down his nose at everyone as if he is so much better than us because he can play golf and the saxophone. He will never admit the fact that his absence in our lives shaped us for the worse. My brothers especially. He's so quick to point out how they need to be better and how ashamed of them that he is as if he was some wonderful role model. He shuns us when we're doing bad, and when any of us succeed at anything, he is the first to claim the credit for our success as if he had a hand in it. It's exhausting and infuriating. He has never done anything for any of us because he couldn't financially. When he did have financial means through his scheme of the month, he opted to wine and dine random women instead of doing something for his family. My father has pretty much always been in my life but has never really been in my life.

My relationship with my father certainly shaped me for the worse but perhaps it also made me better. Sometimes I think about the toxic people that we have in our lives. If we were around them daily and they really had a chance to shape or mold us, would we have turned out any better? If we spent more time around these sort of people, would their traits and issues rub off on us? Maybe it's a blessing in disguise. We can't pick our parents.

If you don't have a father at all, that's ok. No one can replace what a father means to a young woman growing up. Your confidence is affected and so is your self-esteem. The best thing to do is find a "Father figure replacement". Do you have an uncle you look up to? A grandfather, close family friend, stepfather, godfather, or even an older brother? These are all males in your circle who'll be glad to stand in for your absent father. They can give you the love and advice that you need. The "Father figure replacement" is someone who can come into your life and fill that void. You might not have a biological father, but he is the next best thing and he makes it all not so bad. Embrace him today.

2

Parents

"Parents are two imperfect people trying to survive life while raising you to be a decent person."
-Shaleea Venney

Parents are two imperfect people trying to survive life while raising you to be a decent person. They work, go to school, pay the bills, provide the food, shelter and clothing, deal with all the stresses of the day, and still muster up whatever they have left to deal with you. It's hard! There are many who'll tell you there aren't enough hours in one day.

Parents are the foundation of your life. Their work ethic teaches you work ethic. Their loving marriage is a model for the one you want to have one day. When you see your parents reach goals or milestones in their lives, it gives you the confidence to reach yours. Parental units have a lasting effect on you.

With all the good examples that parents show us, are there any bad ones? What if your parents aren't very good role models? I've heard teens say things like "How can they tell me to finish school when they never did?" or "How can they judge me for trying pot, when they did it" or "Why is it wrong that I had sex, when they did the same thing before marriage?" Parents can sometimes come off as being a bit hypocritical when they expect more from you than they achieved themselves. Even if your parents want more from you, understand that they're only telling you these things because they learned the hard way and don't want you to make the same mistakes that they did.

Even if you have horrible parents, they can be amazing teachers if you're paying attention. The same way that your parents' good traits are great examples for you to follow, so are their bad ones. Your parents' examples sometimes show you what to do and, sometimes show you exactly what not to do. There's always a lesson to be learned.

I used to look at my parents' marriage when I was younger and feel sad. My mother always had sad eyes to me. I never saw her truly look happy and I never felt that my father loved her the way she wanted to be loved. I decided that no matter whom I married, he would have to cherish me. I wanted him to look at me as though I was the most beautiful woman in the world and to genuinely cherish me.

My parents never followed their dreams in life. Both had the potential to go anywhere in life they wanted to and did nothing with it. My father had dreams of being a musician and my mother wanted to be a diagnostic sonographer so that she could do the pregnancy ultrasounds. They couldn't be further from where they'd intended today. It sounds funny but the two of them not living out their dreams, caused their lives to be very hard and that inspired me to live my dreams and try to do whatever it took to live an easier life than they did.

Seeing how hard my parents' lives are has taught me to never quit on myself. I want more out of life because of them. I look at them as a blueprint for what not to do in many cases. It's not that my parents are bad people, just people who made bad choices. Did they teach me anything good? Sure they did. Because of them I love the Lord. It is because of my father that I have a love for jazz and books and that I am as cultured as I am. My mother taught me to cook and how to be strong. I don't fault my parents at all. My parents like most of yours, just did the best that they could with what they had, and I thank them.

Whether your parents have been amazing, or they fell short, thank them. Bringing a life into this world and raising them to be the best they can be is no easy feat. I know that some of you may be adopted and if that is the case, you should really take your hats off to them. It takes very special people to love a child that is not theirs biologically as if it were. You are truly blessed to have them.

None of our parents are perfect, but they're ours. With that in mind, do two things more often going forward. Number one, give your parents a break. Number two say thank you. Cut your parents a little slack if you see that they're trying. Start saying thank you more often. There's a misconception that just because they're your parents, they're supposed to do and buy nice things for you. The thought that just because they're your parents, they are obligated to drive you around and you don't need to thank them because it's their job. The law says that your parents are supposed to make sure you are provided for with food, shelter, clothing, and the basics. Nowhere does it say they must purchase expensive cell phones, video games, designer clothes, designer shoes, and takeout food. They don't owe you any of those things. Don't be so entitled that you can't recognize all the hard work they are putting in to give you the things you desire. Not the things you need, the things you want. Parents are people just like everybody else and could use a "Thank you" just like everybody else. Gratitude is a great way to show them they are appreciated. There are lots of absent parents, or people in less fortunate situations than you. It's hard to believe, but it's true. Learn to appreciate.

3

Motherless Daughters

"The sooner you realize and accept who your mother is, the sooner you can allow yourself to forgive her."
-Shaleea Venney

Your relationship with your mother has a great impact on your development. Like your father, she should be there for you and love and encourage you to be the best you can be. The relationship a daughter shares with her mom teaches her a lot about life. Young women tend to emulate their mothers' behavior. Good or bad.

Perhaps you have a working mother whom you feel like you barely see, and your relationship has suffered. Maybe your mother never hugs you or makes you feel like you matter. Some of you have mothers who regret the mistakes they've made in their lives, so they live vicariously through you and that can be a strain. Your mom could be the type to never pay you any attention because she is too enthralled in her relationship with a man. Even worse, are those mothers who suffer from arrested development and don't know how to grow up. They want to be your friend and dress and act like someone half their age. It'd be remiss of me not to mention the mother who has a "Favorite" child (who isn't you) and showers your sibling with love and affection but treats you like the ugly duckling.

The description above that you feel properly depicts your mother doesn't matter. If any of them sound familiar to you, you are a motherless daughter. You didn't get enough encouragement. She didn't prove to you that she cared. She fell asleep behind the wheel that is your life. This is a story that I know all too well. You long for a meaningful relationship with her. You just want her to acknowledge you and tell you how special you are to her.

Mothers are the way they are, for many reasons. They're just people. They're not perfect. They didn't plan on being this kind of mother to you, it just sort of happened. She may not even realize that she treats you the way that she does. She may be suffering from deep depression or bitterness because of a failed relationship. You're close so she's able to take out her frustrations on you. This is especially true if she is a single mother. Single mothers have no choice but to be the mother, the father, the chauffeur, disciplinarian, confidant, provider, and everyday superhuman. It is exhausting! They have no one to help them and their needs, are often last on their own priority list. Remember that, the next time you judge her.

My mother had a strained relationship with her mother. I can tell that she always felt that her mother loved her sisters more than she loved her. I think my mother is an amazing woman and that she loves me. The thing is, she has some deep-rooted hurt from her relationship with her own mother, her current situation, and the regrets she must carry. I think she loves me the best way she knows how.

My mother has been morbidly obese, as far back as I can remember. Because of her size, we were not able to create many mother daughter memories. I used to watch my friends with their mothers and be so jealous at the way they loved and spent time with their daughters. I didn't get many hugs from my mother. She never really told me I was beautiful. No matter how much I succeed in life, she never acts like she is impressed and will quickly change the subject. I have had many accomplishments that I have told my mom about that she did not share with anyone. I'd sometimes talk to my brother or my dad later and be excited to hear their reaction to my good news, only to be disappointed that she never told them. If I am doing bad, or find myself down on my luck, the family knows as soon as she hangs up the phone with me. I have never felt that my heart was *truly* safe with her.

My mother is 300 pounds overweight and so tragically trapped inside of a life that she hates. She had dreams that she did not pursue. I'm not sure why she didn't pursue her dream, but I do have a theory. She gave everything she ever had to be with a man that has never loved her the way she wanted and deserved to be. He's said it himself. He is her number one priority and always was. She was so busy loving him that she didn't really
"Mother" us. I have spent many years even in my adult life seeking her approval, trying to make her proud of me, and trying to make her love me.

Because she has made poor decisions in her life, she is not in a good financial space. Sometimes many days will go by that I don't hear from her and then she'll randomly call me and be like the sweetest mom ever. I always fall for it. That inner child of mine still wants her love. Every time I open up to her, it always ends the same way; she asks me to send her some money or she needs something from me. I die a little bit each time I realize that she was never interested in me at all, but only what I could do for her. It has taken me years to accept that this is the mother I have and that I have no choice but to accept it.

The sooner you realize and accept who your mother is, the sooner you can allow yourself to forgive her. Let go of all anger and openly allow your heart to let her in. She *does* love you. She just has a funny way of showing it.

Those of you, who have doting mothers, be thankful for them. Not everyone can say they have a mother and you may not even realize how much you take her for granted. Being a mother is hard work.

Those of you who have mothers present in your lives please understand who your mother is and who your mother isn't. First and foremost, she is NOT your friend. Secondly, she is your very best friend, confusing right? Let me explain. Your mother is not someone who is there to make life easy, party with you, and let you do as you please, when you please. She should not condone your ridiculous behavior. She should call you out on your crap. She is not your BFF, she is your mother. Although she might be hard on you, remember her tough "Lay down the law" parenting is for your own good. She does it because she wants what's best for you and she has been everywhere you're going. Your mother was a young woman before too. She knows you better than you think. You should never be afraid to tell your mother what is happening in your life out of fear of consequences. Yes, she will be upset at you for making a bad decision or doing whatever you did but, she will ultimately get over it and stand by you throughout the whole ordeal. Because like I said before, she is the best friend you never realized you had. She is always in your corner. She will not turn her back on you. Let her in. Trust her with your heart. It's ok to be vulnerable with your mother. Your secrets absolutely are safe with her.

Still, some of you cannot imagine sharing your hearts with your mothers because they have either broken your trust or have never earned it in the first place. That is ok too. Do you have a "Mother figure replacement?" She might be a cool aunt, an older cousin or sister, a grandmother, one of your mothers' friends, or even a teacher you trust a lot. When you choose your Mother figure replacement, go to her, watch her, use her, and learn from her. Be inspired by her wisdom and her grace and learn everything you can from her. She might not be a permanent fixture in your life for whatever reason but, a strong woman in your life can instill a piece of her strength inside of you that you can always cherish and when she does, try to hold onto it and learn to build on the foundation she started in you.

4

Self-Love/Your Perception

> "The world is full of insecure girls trying to one up each other because the truth is, they're all hopelessly insecure and too terrified to be honest about it."
> -Shaleea Venney

No matter what happens along the way, you must never stop loving yourself. Self- love is downright the most important attribute you can have. People are always going to find something they don't like about you but, what do you think?

You'll always be too tall, too short, too skinny or too chubby. Your hair will be too short or too long. Your skin is too light, or not light enough. Your skin is too dark, or you need a tan. Your breasts will be too small. Your behind won't be big enough. You will never be pretty enough to some people. People will tell you you're too quiet. Others will say that you're too loud, too smart, or too dumb. You're never going to be good enough for everybody. Such is life. All that matters is that you're more than adequate to yourself.

The world is full of insecure girls trying to one up each other because the truth is, they're all hopelessly insecure and too terrified to be honest about it. Beauty is a multi-billion dollar a year industry because of this. Girls are flocking to push it up, squeeze it in, poke it out, cover it up and give the illusion of perfection. Here's something you might not believe: No body is perfect! Learn how to be the perfect you.

There's nothing wrong with wearing makeup or hair extensions as an added compliment to your natural beauty but, if you're all makeup, hair and extras, and your true self is unrecognizable, that's a problem. Beauty products should be an option, not a necessity. Don't become the girl that can't live without her makeup bag out of fear of what others will think of you. If you like makeup that's fine. I never want you to be unable to live without makeup because you think you're unattractive and fear what strangers will think of you. Wipe the makeup off and stare at your beauty. Yes, I said beauty because that's what you are. You are beautiful.

I'll tell you a secret: I never felt insecure about the way that I looked until I compared myself to the way that she looked. Do you ever do that? You walk outside feeling like a supermodel and like you're unstoppable. Your shoes are cute, your jeans look great with the top you're wearing, and your hair's on point! You look in the mirror and feel ready for the day. Somewhere during your day, you run into "Miss America" who has perfect legs and perfect hair. Her smile lights up the room. Suddenly, you need to lose weight. As a matter of fact, your outfit isn't as well put together as you thought. Your hair! Look at how dull it looks, it doesn't even shine and it's not flowing like hers. What started out as a great day has now turned into an unconstructive, self-criticize party. Why do we this? Why can't you both be equally beautiful? Why do we have to compare ourselves to each other? Is it not possible that both of you can be beautiful? The next time you find yourself feeling insecure and comparing yourself to another girl, stop and do one thing: Tell her how pretty you think she is! I know, it sounds crazy! You'd be surprised how satisfying it is to tell another girl that you think that she is beautiful and guess what, it will take nothing away from you. It will catch her off guard and it is very freeing for you. When you let go of the envy you feel and transform it into kind words, it helps both of you. Somehow, your knowing that she was beautiful, distracted you from the idea that so are you. When we compliment other women on their appearances, it boosts our moods along with theirs. If we could learn to stop being in competition with one another, we wouldn't be so hateful. It's not a competition. Don't ever be intimidated by another woman's light, you have your own.

Confidence is the key. Knowing who you are makes you less fazed by who everyone else wants you to be. You must learn to recognize what works for you and what doesn't. Confidence can be seen from a mile away. When you like yourself, others will like you as well. People will gravitate towards you. Self-love has nothing to do with your looks, it's all about how you feel about yourself. No matter if you weigh a buck ten or three hundred and fifty pounds, you look in the mirror and can honestly say "I *really* like me" and mean it!

The reason why it's called self-love is because it's all about the love you have for yourself. Never let anyone else convince you that you are less than. Eleanor Roosevelt once said, "No one can make you feel inferior without your consent". Simply put, you have the control over what you think and feel about yourself. People are always going to talk about you, but you need to brush it off and not take any of it to heart. When we internalize what others think and say about us, we begin to believe their lies. Thus, giving others the consent to make us feel inferior. The only critic that should matter is you.

Today I want you to do one thing. Take your clothes off and stand in front of the mirror. What do you see? Pay special attention to your belly, your thighs, your arms. Everything you hate about yourself. Turn to the side and look at it from different angles. Stare at it all. Now. STOP frowning and cringing about everything that is wrong with your body. There is nothing wrong with your body. Your body functions exactly the way it is supposed to. You can see and hear. You can walk, run, sit, stand, and anything else you physically want to do. Realize that there are millions of disabled people who are unable to do most of those things you take for granted. If you stop looking at your body as an object and start to appreciate it for everything it does for you each day, your way of thinking will change. Your body is beautifully designed and functional. Embrace your flaws and, if you can't embrace the flaws yet, focus solely on what you do like about yourself. Speak positive thoughts about yourself. The more you hear it, the more you will believe it. Allow the positive confessions to catch on until it's natural.

    You are a gem my dear. Gems can't help but shine no matter what. Shine on.

5

Periods: Toxic Shock Syndrome

"Pay close attention to when you insert your tampon because they need to be changed regularly just like pads. Don't forget you are wearing one."
-Shaleea Venney

One day you'll be minding your own business trying to make it through your day when you'll get a visit from an uninvited guest. Mother Nature! Tah-dah! You my friend have just landed head first into the beginning of womanhood. Don't be afraid.

You may suddenly feel "wet" down there. You might go to the restroom and discover blood in your underwear. It can be scary and nerve wracking but, if you're prepared, you'll be fine.

Puberty is the time in your life when you are becoming a woman. You'll start to develop breasts. Some girls start puberty at ages 9-12 and others may be late bloomers who start between 13 and 14. We are all different and all our bodies will go through puberty at their own paces. There's nothing wrong with starting early and there's nothing wrong with you if you're the last of all your friends to get yours.

While it is very hard to pinpoint when you'll get your first period, most girls begin theirs about 2 to 2½ years after breast development starts. Some get it sooner than that. The best way to grasp an idea of when Mother Nature is almost ready to make her grand appearance is when you notice a discharge coming from your vagina. This discharge could be thin and sticky or thick and gooey. It might be white, or an off- white color. You'll notice it on your underwear when you use the restroom. You may also start growing hair down there and under your arms. If this has started happening already, your period is probably less than a year or so from happening.

But what is a period? What is happening to your body? As a girl, you have 2 ovaries which are filled with thousands of tiny little eggs and two fallopian tubes. Your fallopian tubes connect your ovaries to your uterus or womb. This is the place where you will one day grow a baby. Every month, your body gets prepared for the possibility of carrying a child. When you are in between periods, the walls of your uterus get very thick with blood and tissue because if you conceive a baby, it will need to be surrounded by soft cushion while it grows. Your uterus waits on your ovaries to release the egg and once the egg arrives unfertilized by sperm (you did not have sexual intercourse where a man ejaculated into you and his sperm met with your egg) the uterus quickly realizes that it is not making a baby and therefore, has no use for the extra blood and tissue it stored so it releases it through your vagina. This is your period in a nutshell.

Periods can last from 2-3 days to a week. Some of your friends will tell you theirs is very heavy meaning they experience lots of bloody discharge. Some women get very bad cramps. Some start off heavy and get lighter as they go on. Everybody is different. Don't be surprised if you get your first period and then don't have another one for months. This is normal. We have all had "irregular" periods.

No matter how your period starts, you need to be informed. Don't get caught out there unprepared. This is where your sanitary napkins A.K.A pads come in handy. Always keep a pad in your backpack or purse. You never know when it could start, and you want to be safe, not sorry. Pads are designed with sticky adhesive on the bottom of them to stick to your undies. You simply pull down your undies, remove the sticker from the bottom of your pad, place the sticky side on top of your underwear, and pull your underwear back up. Done! Pads come in different sizes and lengths and will say things like heavy, light days, or panty liners on the boxes. My favorite is the one that is labeled "wings" on the box. These give you an added sense of protection because they have an extra piece of material on each side of them that is made to go around your undies to prevent any blood from seeping onto your panties (where your thighs meet). Pads are designed to cover you no matter how light or heavy your period is. You should change your pad about every 3 hours, but this will vary depending on how much bloody discharge you are experiencing. When you change your pad, NEVER flush it down the toilet. Remove it, wrap it in tissue, and drop it in the little box found next to the toilet inside of almost every public or school restroom stall, or in the wastebasket.

You may opt to use tampons when you get your period. Tampons are just like pads, but they go inside of your vagina. It's very important to learn how to insert a tampon for the first time. Try inserting it on a day when you're having a normal – heavy flow because the more discharge you are having the easier it is to insert. Look for those with rounded top applicators they're very easy to use. Always go with the most- slender size you can find when you are just starting out using them. Tampons have strings at the bottom of them that hang out of your vagina so that you can easily pull them to remove it. Pay close attention to when you insert your tampon because they need to be changed regularly just like pads. Don't forget you are wearing one.

There is a very serious condition called **Toxic Shock Syndrome** (TSS) that you can develop if you do not remove your tampon in a timely manner. According to the Mayoclinic.com and Wikipedia, Toxic shock syndrome is a condition caused by bacterial toxins most commonly due to Staphylococcus infection. These toxins build up inside you and can be life threatening. The symptoms of TSS are fever greater than 102 F, vomiting, diarrhea, low blood pressure, seizures, headache, a red sunburn looking rash that covers most of your body, headache, muscle aches, and sore throat. If you acquire TSS, it can be treated with medications like antibiotics, with medical procedures such as drainage, or amputation, and through intravenous or oxygen therapies. No need to panic, be informed, be diligent, and change your tampon regularly. NO! Tampons cannot get lost inside of you and yes you can still pee when you are wearing one. Don't worry. If you're still unsure of which option is best for you talk to your mother, school nurse or any older woman you trust. We all get them and it's nothing to be scared about. You're just growing up. Congratulations.

6

The Boy/Don't Settle For the First Guy Who Looks At You

> "Understand this, if a guy is really into you, he will genuinely want what's best for you."
> -Shaleea Venney

One day you will be minding your own business and BOOM out of nowhere, the boy will come waltzing into your life and it will turn your world upside down. It happens to all of us and it's a normal part of life. Remember that you are a beautiful girl.

More importantly than your beauty, I would ask for you to remember that you are special. The thing about boys is that they're boys. Boys are all about the chase growing up. They are very likely to mature slower than we do as girls. While your intentions may be admirable, theirs are usually not. Most boys are looking to charm and hook up with as many girls as possible. It's just how it goes. You need to be confident enough to not fall for the first guy who tells you you're attractive. Find out his intentions. Does he have a reputation for being a player? Have you seen him with lots of girls? What have you heard about him? I would never advise you to make unfair assumptions about someone before you know him, but usually where there's smoke there's fire. If you've heard that he's trouble, he more than likely is. Tread carefully.

Understand that you are special. You must carry yourself as if the sun rises and sets on you, because it should. Am I suggesting you to be arrogant or a narcissist? Not at all. If you believe you are special, young men will believe it too. Let's be clear, as ladies, we must not believe that all the fault is on us. The same way that you should be respectful, is the same way, that parents should be teaching their sons to respect you. Young men are just as responsible for their actions as we are for ours. We cannot control the way that we are treated by the opposite sex, and there will be jerks out there no matter what we do but, the way a young man treats you is largely based on the way you carry yourself. If you carry yourself like a respectable young woman, you are more likely to be treated as such. Guys can tell that a girl is "easy" right away and they will capitalize off their suspicions given the opportunity.

Many young men will approach you but, you can't fall hard and ride off into the sunset with each one of them. Accept the compliments, smile, and keep it moving. You must not be fazed by every guy who tells you you're beautiful. You already know that you are beautiful. Don't be so easily impressed by simple words, look at actions. Guys are telling all the girls they are beautiful, and the ones that don't know that they are special, fall for the hype and end up with bad reputations because they fall prey to the sweet words of every guy. Never forget how special you are, and never let any guy try to convince you that you are average. Your self-esteem and confidence are necessary when dealing with the opposite sex. If he isn't willing to treasure you and treat like you are one in a million, then wait until you find the guy that will.

It's highly unlikely that you will find your soulmate this young. Don't get me wrong, it is possible, but those couples are the exception, not the rule. I tell you this because it is very important for you to understand the nature of the relationship going in. Date guys, have fun, but don't go overboard. Should you go to the movies and out to eat? Absolutely. Should you take off your underwear and climb into bed with him? No! Dating, should be like a close friendship. You hang out and go places together and sometimes you may kiss. It doesn't have to be more than this and I don't care how hard society tries to tell you otherwise.

This is the reason why you must understand the nature of the relationship going in. What is your guy *really* here for? Does he genuinely like being with you and enjoy your company? Is he pressuring you for more? More could mean making you neglect your studies, breaking rules at home such as curfew, or making you do things that you wouldn't normally do to impress him. If you ever have to pretend to be someone else, or do things that you are uncomfortable doing, this is not the right guy and he doesn't like you for you, he likes you for who he can mold you into.

Understand this, if a guy is really into you, he will genuinely want what's best for you. He will not put you into tough situations. You both need to have a balance that includes spending time with each other but, also not neglecting your primary responsibilities such as school, or things that you are responsible for at home. The ideal guy will help you to be better in some way and will hold you accountable as well. For the sake of argument, let's say you're an amazing student. You have straight A's and are a high achiever. You let your grades slip a little bit here and there, and don't study as much anymore which results in your grades taking a dive. Your guy finds out. What does he say? Is he upset at you for letting this happen? Does he act like it's no big deal and continue to demand lots of your time? Perhaps he offers to study with you? How he responds to your problems matters. Is he trying to help you to get back up, or is he aware that you have slipped some and is willing to stand idly by while it's happening? It matters. What kind of guy is your guy?

There is nothing wrong with you liking a boy. Parents only dislike the idea because we know what liking a boy could potentially lead to- we'll discuss this more later. If you must like a boy, please try to make an informed decision. By informed decision I simply mean actually taking your time getting to know the guy you say you like. Is he religious? Is he kind hearted? Does he have a father in his life? How does he treat his mother and sisters? What are his habits? All these things matter. Kindness matters. It matters how he treats others around him. Is he nice to others? You don't want to be tied to the bully. If he has a father in his life, this will greatly shape the kind of man he is becoming. His father will show him strength, and how to love a woman. He will show him how to be a man. He will teach him how to dress, and shave, and give him confidence. He will be someone he can go to for advice.

How he treats his mother and sisters is huge. You should be able to tell that he loves and respects his mother and sisters. He should be protective of their hearts. If you know that he curses his mother out and disrespects her, this should not be a good sign for you. If he would treat his mother- the woman who gave him life- as anything less than that, how will he treat you? If you've seen him call his mother out of her name, don't be surprised when he calls you out of yours.

Take your time my dear. Take your time with dating and figuring things out. There is no need to rush into anything. Date or don't date. Whatever you decide to do, it is your decision. Don't let any friend, or boy influence you in any way. You must trust yourself and listen to your gut. Boys aren't going anywhere anytime soon. When you're ready, they'll be there. You are in control. Don't forget that.

7

Cold Porcelain/Losing Your Virginity

"Why am I telling you such intimate details of my life? I need it to be real for you."
-Shaleea Venney

I'll tell you a secret that only one other person knows. I fell hard for this guy when I was 13. I was sure that I was going to love him forever and there was nothing anyone could tell me that would make me change my mind. He had curly hair, hazel colored oval shaped eyes, he was slim with an athletic build like a basketball player, and he stood at 5'11". His skin was smooth and an umber, dark yellow-brown. He had full lips and his face was devastatingly handsome. So smooth, I could smell his confidence in the air when he passed me. He was tall dark and handsome and he knew it. He was so much cooler than I could ever hope to be. We were young kids who were infatuated with each other. We'd walk to go and get ice cream and just hang out. My parents didn't mind too much because for one, we were young and harmlessly talking, and for two, he lived far away and was only there for the summer visiting his family. Both of us wanted to spend as much time as we could together. The fact that we both knew that our summer love would end soon led us to rush into things that neither of us were ready for. One day, we were talked into "hooking up" by his older cousin.

    He was visiting his cousin for the entire summer and his cousin lived just down the block from me. I went to his cousins' house to see him one day and heard his older cousin announce that "Today would be the day". I wasn't sure what he meant. We were sitting in his cousins bedroom talking with the door open, when in walks his older cousin to hand my guy a condom. My heart began racing and I felt my face turn flush. My heart was beating so loudly, I was sure they could hear it. I was terrified! Here is a guy that I hadn't even open mouth kissed. Sure, we'd kissed, but I'd never even stuck my tongue out when we'd kissed because I was too afraid I'd be bad at it and I didn't want to be embarrassed. Now, I was supposed to have sex with him? Here, in his cousins bedroom that smelled like musty t-shirts, with walls littered with Sports Illustrated bikini pictures, on a twin mattress? I was totally panicking. He shut the door, looked at me, and said "You know we don't have to do this right?" "Oh, thank God!" I thought on the inside while shyly staring into his eyes. Finally, when the silence was so awkward it became unbearable, I told him that I was scared and didn't know if I wanted to do this-today. He looked at me and said "Me either. Plus, I don't want to hurt you, it's supposed to hurt when girls lose their virginity". At that very moment, his aunt came home, noticed the bedroom door was closed, and began banging on the door asking us to come out right away. When we opened the door, she sensed something was off and questioned "What are you doing?" in an accusatory tone that made it clear she knew exactly *what* we were doing. "Get out of here right now!" she yelled at us, and we ran out of there as quickly as we could.

    In the days and months that followed, summer ended, he went home, and he and I continued to talk on the phone having a long-distance relationship. He was attractive and far away, I knew he was talking to other girls, even though I was only thinking of him. Then one day, just like that, we had this huge fight over the phone, and he was such a jerk to me. I'm not even sure what we fought about now but, I can still remember him telling me something to the tone of "You don't matter to me, and I have lots of girls out here". His words stung. I hung up the phone and I never spoke to him again after that day. I remember being so thankful that I didn't lose my virginity to him.

    About a year later, I was at home hanging out with my brothers and their neighborhood friends. My brothers were friends with everybody in the neighborhood and everyone was into music. Lots of evenings they'd hang out in the stairwell of our apartment building and sing and rap and just laugh together. Every single one of my brothers' friends had hit on me at some point and I'd turn them all down at one point or another. One evening, a new face was added to the mix. I knew all the guys from the neighborhood because of my brothers but, this guy wasn't someone I was familiar with. He rode up on a bicycle and everyone seemed to know him. He stayed downstairs and hadn't even come inside of the front gate when he and I made eye contact for the first time. I was standing up looking down from the second-floor stairwell and my brothers and their buddies were all sitting beneath me on the first floor in the stairwell. He grabbed his bike, opened the front gate, and came inside of the building. I could hear him downstairs below me asking his friends "who's the girl?" they all laughed and said "Man! Don't even try".

    He made his way to the second floor where I was sitting and sat down with an air of confidence. He was tall. Towering over me, he stood over 6 feet. He too, was thin and athletically built like a basketball player. His face was not round, it was long. He had very large lips, and a big nose. His eyes! I fell in love with his eyes the first time I saw him. They were dark brown and almond shaped. I loved how they fit his face. There was this warmth and kindness in his eyes that drew me to him. When I looked into his eyes, it felt like I had known him forever. Something about the way he looked at me was… different. I could tell right away. He wore black Nike sneakers, blue jeans, and a Marshall Faulk NFL jersey. I was instantly intrigued by him. We exchanged names and shy smiles. He later told me that all his friends told him not to even try to talk to me. I laughed, looked at him, and asked "What does that mean?" to which he replied without skipping a beat, "That I'm going to try anyway". Just like that, he left. I was so bummed out. We had this brief conversation and he asked me my name, told me he would try to talk to me, and left! Turns out, he had only gone to the store to get some juice and licorice. When he came back, we all sat, talked, and hung out as a group. This was the first time I had ever seen him. This was the last time, I would ever go a day without seeing him.

We were fast friends. I saw him every day going forward after the day we met on the stairs. He'd come over to see my brothers and stop and talk to me. We'd quietly flirt. Our friendship felt so natural. Neither of us knew what was happening but we both knew *something* was happening. I couldn't tell my brothers because he was their friend. I couldn't tell my parents because he was older than me, and he was the school jock and I was the school nerd. There was no way my dad who had been grooming me to marry Tiger Woods, would accept me dating the guy from around the way. So, we kept it to ourselves. This whole "sneak to see each other" routine went on for a year. We'd talk on the phone for hours. He was my first real-stick your tongue out- kiss. I was so nervous to kiss him because I was afraid I'd be bad at it. He was older and more experienced than me. He would always ask me to give him a "real kiss" so one day I did. He kind of chuckled as if he knew I had never done this before and hugged me tightly.

One day I got this random call from him. He basically told me that he had "Needs" and that if I really cared about him like he cared about me, that I would be willing to "Do it". He said that we'd been talking for over a year and he really cared about me but, I needed to understand his plight. One day a few weeks later, he came to our house in the middle of the night and it happened. My parents both worked nights and my brothers weren't paying attention, so he was able to come by. We went to the only place we could go- the bathroom. I remember sitting on the toilet trembling with fear and him telling me to "Hold me tight". I lost my virginity on the toilet in our small bathroom. When he left, I went into the living room, turned on the floor fan, and laid on the couch with my legs open in front of it trying to cool down the burning sensation that I felt down there. It was stinging, burning, and bleeding a little. I had just lost my virginity. I didn't know how to feel about it or if I'd even see him again. I would always hear about guys getting what they wanted from you and never coming back. I was worried.

We continued to talk after this and he didn't leave me as I had feared he might've if I'd had sex with him.

Why am I telling you such intimate details of my life? I need it to be real for you. I want you to know that I did not wait until I was married to have sex. I'm not proud of that but, it is my truth.

Perhaps you can learn something from my experience.

The first time I almost had sex, was because of pressure from someone else, and thank goodness, we didn't. Imagine if I had. I had strong feelings for him. What if we'd have had sex and when he got back home and switched up on me, I had already given him my virginity? I would've been devastated. When I did have sex, I had been seeing my guy for a year and six months exactly. We had sex, and I was sure that I loved him. Was I *really* ready though? Would I have wanted to have sex if he hadn't suggested we do? Probably not. My feelings for him weren't going anywhere, and I was fine with waiting. So why did I do it? Sometimes, we do things, we wouldn't usually do, when we like someone or think we are in love. I was sure I was in love with him. I was just a baby, what did I really know about being in love.

I want you to be careful. You must guard your heart and your virginity. It might not be precious to everybody else, but it should be precious to you. If you give it to the wrong guy, you will never be able to get it back. Don't let anyone make you do anything you don't want to do. Guys will try to convince you to do it with slick lines like "Everybody else is doing it, if you really loved me you'd do it, the other girls are willing to do it, I can get it from someone else, and I love you". Don't let him fool or threaten you with any of this. If he really loves you, his love shouldn't have an expiration date if you don't have sex with him. He should respect your desire to wait. He shouldn't pressure you or make you feel guilty about it. I know you're thinking, how could I tell you any of this when I didn't wait? That is precisely the reason, hindsight is always 20/20. There is no better teacher than real life experience. I would hate for you to have sex with one guy whom you think you care for and that his feelings are mutual, only to be left alone once he gets what he wants. Guys do this all the time. It's so important to choose carefully. If I had it to do over, perhaps I would have waited. Perhaps I wouldn't have lost something so important to me in a cramped bathroom, on cold porcelain.

8

Teenage Motherhood/Sex

> "Girls, when you have a baby, YOU have a baby."
> -Shaleea Venney

I told you how I lost my virginity. What I didn't tell you is that I lost more than my virginity on that cold porcelain. I lost my innocence that night, but I also lost the rest of my youth. The first time I ever had sex, I also became a mother unbeknownst to me.

Can you just imagine what this is like? The first time you have sex, you get pregnant! I didn't know anything was wrong at first. One day out of nowhere, I started throwing up. I'm not one to throw up or really even get sick at all for that matter but, I didn't think anything of it. The nausea wouldn't subside. Still, I didn't think anything of it. I remember being at school with my friends, when one of them suggested I take a pregnancy test. I had never even considered this could be the source of my illness. My friends bought a test for me and the next day we tested my urine at lunch time and it was positive. I felt my heart stop inside of my chest.

I prayed and prayed that the test was wrong. I bargained with God, that if He would just not let me be pregnant, I would serve Him forever and be the best Christian alive. None of this worked. I spoke with an older neighbor who convinced me to go to the clinic to get a blood test to confirm the results and that I needed to tell the father of my unborn child. She gave me a ride to the clinic she had suggested and they too confirmed what I already knew, I was going to be a mother. The nurses felt sorry for me. I was so young. They wanted to do an ultrasound and encouraged me to call the father of the baby so that he could be a part of it too. We were still talking to each other, and he'd told me he loved me, so I thought it would be safe to invite him for the ultrasound. I called him, and he drove right over-with a friend. I met him in the clinic lobby and he couldn't believe our new circumstances. We were going to be parents. He brought the least serious person he knew with him. It turns out, they were already hanging out nearby and when I called him, he came right over. This was so embarrassing to me because I didn't expect him to bring anyone and I didn't want anyone to know. His friend cracked jokes and tried to make light of the heavy situation.

We got the ultrasound together and the staff gave us parenting tips, advice, and even videos to help us try and get prepared. The whole time, I was trying to read him for any signs of anger, or happiness, or fear. Just ANYTHING. He kept his poker face the whole time. When we had a moment alone, he looked me in the eye, squeezed my hands tightly, and kissed my forehead ever so gently. He asked "Is this really happening?" in a calm but nervous tone. He took the news better than I expected but, he was obviously trying to adjust to the news of his newfound fatherhood.

I couldn't tell my parents. I was terrified. I contemplated running away, abortion, and being a single mother if he didn't choose to stick around for our baby. I felt like I was living in a mental prison. I had no one I could tell. I didn't even tell my best friend Dolly because I was so embarrassed at the idea that I could really be in such a situation. It was such a lonely time for me.

He had a very close relationship with his mother. She was very fond of me from the first time I met her about a year before all of this. I remember the first time I met her. She was carrying in groceries and he said "I want you to meet my mom". He walked me into her bedroom and told me to relax because he could hear my heart beating out of my chest behind him. He said "Mom I want you to meet Shaleea". She smiled the biggest, sweetest, smile and said "She's BEAUTIFUL! and you're not so bad yourself son!" She hugged me and said "I like you already".

He convinced me that we should talk to her about the baby and since I knew she liked me, I agreed. She was in our corner right away and was strongly against the idea of abortion. I remember her hugging me and telling me it would be "Ok" like only she could. It was a huge weight off our shoulders to have the support from a parent. His mother was amazing. She was always genuine, and honest. She was the life of the party. She kept everything and everyone together. She could be strong when she needed to be, and as gentle as she had to be. She was a no nonsense, tell it like it is kind of woman. I both feared and coveted her strength. I respected her. I adored her. We had a beautiful bond.

After our discussion, it was decided that she would help us break the news to my parents. I'll never forget her standing in my parents' living room telling them in a matter of fact tone that "We're going to be grandparents". My parents didn't take the news well and immediately called for me to abort the baby because they were sure that my guy was not in it for the long run, and my future was ruined. His mother, stood her ground and politely informed my parents that "My son is in love with your daughter, wants to be a father to their child, and to be there for your daughter and the baby they made together". My parents had no choice but to get on board with the idea that I was having a baby because California law said that they had no right to force me to terminate the pregnancy.

Although my parents had no choice but to let me have the baby, that still didn't mean they'd welcome her father with open arms. In fact, my father was adamant that he didn't want "That boy" in his house. My mother eventually came around because she figured that if they pushed away the father, I would inevitably become the single mother they were so desperately trying to prevent me from becoming. They slowly but surely started allowing him to come and visit me, bring me food, and spend time with me and our unborn child. When the time finally came for me to give birth, we were all one big reluctantly happy family.

He had taken a job to help plan for the baby so when I went into labor, he took off work and was there with me every step of the way. Turns out I was only two centimeters dilated and was sent home to wait. The very next day, I was sure I was going to have her again, but both sets of our parents advised him to go to work because he didn't need to miss work 2 days in a row. He went to work. I, of course, went into labor, for real this time. I was in the worst pain of my life. It wouldn't subside no matter what I did. I called his mother on the way to the hospital.

My mom and my uncle who was also our neighbor, drove me to the hospital. I remember running down the halls of the labor and delivery department looking for an empty room I could go into to wait for the doctor. The nurse came in, assessed my cervix, and announced that we were going to have a baby because I was 3 cm dilated. My doctor, who coincidentally happened to be at the hospital delivering another baby, came into my room to see how I was doing. At that moment, my mother grabbed her phone and walked out into the hallway to call my dad and the rest of the family, to let everyone know I was going to be admitted and a baby would be there soon.

My doctor asked me how I was I doing, and I told him that I was 3 cm dilated and doing ok. He opted to check me out for himself and after he did, things went very quickly. When he checked me, he told me I was fully dilated, and needed to start pushing. I was so scared. My abdomen and stomach felt as though I was having a bowel movement and needed to bear down. My body was bearing down automatically without any effort from me. I was trying to breathe but couldn't catch my breath to do so because of the pain and the involuntary bearing down. I kept hearing the doctor and my mother yelling at me to "BREATHE". Out of nowhere, my hospital room was full of nursing staff and doctors surrounding me. I knew something was very wrong. I wasn't getting enough oxygen and because I wasn't getting enough air, neither was she. The medical team was worried that one or both of us may not make it. They applied an oxygen mask to my face. With a sense of urgency and determination, I pushed with all my might until I felt her come out of me. Once her head came out, it's like the pain intensity decreased. I could still feel the pain, but it was really a relief knowing she was almost fully here. The doctors immediately grabbed her and ran to the prepped area on the other side of the room to work on her. I didn't hear anything for what felt like an eternity, and then finally, I heard my baby cry out. I cried too. They brought her over and I examined her tiny 5 lb 12 oz body for any signs of anything being wrong with her. She was perfect. Besides the fact that the skin on her bottom and back was purplish blue, she was perfect. The doctors educated me on the fact that her back discoloration was due to the lack of oxygen she sustained during the delivery and that it would dissipate. The nurse put her on my bare skin so that we could bond. I stared at her sweet little face for as long as I could. She was beautiful.

    Her dad walked in shortly after her birth and was so saddened that he had missed it by a few minutes, that he laid his head on my chest and softly sobbed repeating that he was sorry. The two of them were instant besties. As soon as she heard his voice she smiled and wrapped her entire little hand around his pointer finger. They were in love with each other right from the start. I'll never forget how he wanted to stay up and stare at her the night she was born. I was completely exhausted and only wanted to sleep.

When we got home from the hospital, the baby and I spent half the time at my parents' house and the other half at his moms' house. We didn't have the ideal living situation but, we made it work.

Consequences and Repercussions….

I'd had a baby. I was still a kid myself. It was hard. I had a great support system, but it was still hard. I had to drop out of school to take care of the baby. I didn't see my friends much anymore. Most of their mothers saw me as the bad seed and a bad influence because I'd had a baby. That hurt me the most. Most of my friends were having sex before me and had multiple partners, but I was now the bad seed for getting pregnant by my boyfriend. It was very sobering how lonely things got for me. I spent all day in the house with a baby. It seemed like everyone else was living life and having fun, and I couldn't because I had a little person to think about. I missed parties, the prom, high school graduation, senior ditch day, grad night, hanging at the mall with my friends and pretty much every other teenage milestone you can think of.

Girls, when you have a baby, YOU have a baby. How many times have you seen a couple have a baby and the mother is pretty much the one who takes care of the baby full time? It's true. While I will never discredit her father for being there for me, he was a teenage guy. He still wanted to do what teenage guys do. There were many days that he was out hanging out with his friends, or other girls while I was home with our baby. I spent countless days feeling like I was alone and regretting having a baby so young. I was smart. I was supposed to go to Spain to study abroad. I had my whole life to look forward to. What had I done?

Exactly 3 years later, when I was 19, we welcomed a son into our family. We continued to struggle with our growing family and we both took odd jobs to help our family. We continued to live with our parents. I'd had 2 babies out of wedlock before I was 20.

It is a miracle that we were able to make it work at such a young age. Neither of us knew what we were doing but we made it through. We had lots of friends who found themselves in similar situations who did not make it. It is not my hope that you find yourself in this sort of situation.

Understand that you should never have a baby with the hopes that it will force a guy to stay with you. Quite the contrary, if a guy doesn't want you, he doesn't want you. Please don't try to get pregnant thinking that the baby will somehow make him want or love you. It won't. A guy can be fully present in your child's life and still not have anything to do with you romantically.

If you are having trouble romantically with your guy, please don't be the girl who thinks that having a baby will "fix" your relationship. Here's the secret that most people won't tell you: When you have a baby, your relationship becomes more strained. Raising a little person is hard work. Between sleep deprivation, crying, school, and working while trying to make ends meet, you'll be so emotionally exhausted that it can often hurt your relationship if it's not built on a solid foundation. I have married friends who are successful, fully functioning adults. Some of them have had to stop working for a while to stay home with the baby while their husbands work. These women are used to working and being able to come and go as they please. Babies change all of that. The resentment that some of them felt for their husbands who got to get up, go to work, and have a break from the screaming baby all day blew me away but, it's a normal feeling and doesn't make any of them bad mothers. It's tough raising a baby. There are wives who are the only ones getting up at night with the babies because their husbands leave it to them because they have work in the morning. They are angry, and exhausted and even though they know their spouses are busy, human nature still can't help but feel overwhelmed. This can lead to very big arguments. These are grown people.

Add up all the struggle the successful married couples deal with and multiply it with immaturity, selfishness, narcissism, arrested development, financial barriers, peer pressure, fear of missing out on teenage milestones, partying, drinking, studying, cheating, and everything else teenagers deal with. Do you see the problem? Do you really believe that you're equipped with the emotional tools needed to handle it? Having a baby will not make him love you more and bring you closer. It might do more harm than good. Really think about your reasoning for wanting to have a baby. Do you really want to be a teen mother and a single parent?

9

Promiscuity

"Ladies: You can't fill your empty spaces by having random guys fill your private spaces."
-Shaleea Venney

You are a young lady and you should carry yourself as such. No matter what you may have seen on social media, what the feminists say, or how many "slut walks" they put on year after year, being promiscuous is NOT cute. Sleeping with lots of different men is not "freeing". It is not you "owning your sexual experience". It is not ok to sleep around because "the boys do it, so girls can too". I never want you to be that girl. Be respectable. Am I saying that young promiscuous ladies have no respect for themselves? Am I "slut shaming?" Yes! Absolutely.

When my generation was growing up, it was not cool to be the fast girl. No one took that girl seriously. The guys would say "You can't turn a hoe into a housewife". Would they sleep with the girl? Sure! Would they seriously make her their wife and start a family with her? Heck no! Now, guys are literally marrying strippers. The times we are living in today probably have tricked you into thinking that you need to be about that life because it's all around you.

Today if you call a girl out for the things she is doing or what she is wearing, you are "slut shaming". It's hilarious how society has taught us that we are the ones with the problem for calling it out, more than the girl is for her actions.

Ladies with respect for themselves carry themselves to a certain standard. The image you put out of yourself matters. What are you posting on social media? If I went through your posts would I find pictures you were ashamed of? Would you be ok with your dad seeing the things you posted online? What about a Pastor? If you're a good girl, the way you speak, act, post, and dress should coincide with that.

The reason that some of these girls post naked twerking pictures online, is the same reason some girls are promiscuous: For attention. Perhaps they never felt they were enough, they think their bodies are all they have to offer, or they want to be liked. Sweetheart, if you are doing any of these things in the hopes of being liked or taken seriously, you are painfully wrong in your approach. You don't have to give away too much, it's ok to keep some mystery.

It's so important to just be you. Trying to be something you're not, will turn you into something you're not. If you're a good girl and start dressing and acting sexier for the attention of the opposite sex, don't be surprised when he wants you to back up all those sexy actions for real. When you advertise sex, guys don't believe that you are falsely advertising, they want a sexual rendezvous. When you talk the talk, people believe that you walk the walk. The walk might not be something you're really ready for. Some guy will call your bluff, and there's a chance that you're likely to do whatever he wants you to out of fear of abandonment. He then gets what he wants, leaves you hurting, and you continue to repeat the cycle. Now you have a bad reputation. "Bad" girls don't just walk right into bad reputations, they're mostly good girls who ended up in bad circumstances due to poor choices.

When you advertise your body, please don't be shocked when someone wants to rent it. I use the word rent on purpose because most people don't want to buy something they can get for free. The problem with advertising your body is that it leads guys to only want one thing from you: Your body. There's not a ton of interest in getting to know the real you. They only want the piece of you that you advertised. They may even request it multiple times. Don't get confused when he calls you for more later. It's so important that you don't confuse being wanted with being important. Just because a guy will sleep with you doesn't mean he values you. Be careful. He's mostly there because you give yourself away for free and it's easy. Everybody likes getting something for free, even if it's cheap. You don't value yourself and he learned how to treat you from YOU. You're still just someone that he uses and calls when he wants sex because he knows that you're going to be available. He sees you as an easy conquest because you have presented yourself in such a way.

Some girls will even try to convince you that they sleep around for themselves because they love sex. One thing wrong with that statement; you can love sex with one person. You can be in a healthy relationship and have lots of sex with that person. Hopping in and out of the bed of every guy you meet is not productive, not safe, and plain out nasty. You have baggage and need professional help to understand why. Ladies: *You can't fill your empty spaces by having random guys fill your private spaces.* Sex is not the way to fill your loneliness or your need to feel worthy. It lasts a few moments, and then it's over and you're back to square one.

One day you will find that special someone who is worthy of you and everything you have to offer, and it'll be special. It'll feel right. Don't give your body away to everybody. You deserve more than being some guys' one-night stand. You are worth more than your assets.

One of the best ways to not be promiscuous, is to not be promiscuous. Go against the grain. There are lots of easy girls out there, be different. If you find a guy you like, don't sleep with him. Just try it. When lots of the other girls are easy, and you give a guy a challenge, he doesn't know how to react, he is intrigued. He finds himself wanting to figure you out. Make a guy take the time to get to know you. If a guy is trying to get what he wants from you, but you won't give it to him, he has 2 choices: He can either stop seeing you because he feels you're not worth it, or keep seeing you because you've piqued his interest. Before he knows what has happened, he has developed some sort of real feelings for you even if it's a friendship. At the very least, he will have to respect you. This is not to play games or to "trick" a guy into falling for you, the point is to force a guy to take a real look at you and to see you as more than your lady parts. You don't need to sleep with a guy for him to like you and if you do, he's the wrong guy.

Being respectable will never go out of style. Holding yourself to a higher standard is always a good idea. You should be courted. Flowers, dates, and real phone calls, are not old school, they are things a guy does to show you that you are special. You must demand the best, because it is what you deserve.

Protection, Protection, Protection…

I would never be a hypocrite and say wait till you're married but if you must have sex, please protect yourself. Always wear a condom, use birth control, and be in control of your body and your sexual choices. There are more things to worry about than pregnancy. You are at risk of contracting a bevy of sexually transmitted infections (STI). You can get rid of some but others, could be with you for the rest of your life, and could be life threatening. The rule to know is that when you have sex, you have sex with everyone the person you are having sex with had sex with. If the person you're having sex with has had 5 partners, how many have each of them had, and each of their partners? Before you know it, the list can be massive. When you take in to account the fact that most people that have STIs are not aware that they have an STI, it's even more important to protect yourself. This also applies to oral sex. Some of you are having oral sex because you think it's safer. You may not get pregnant via oral methods, but you are still susceptible to STIs via the semen and vaginal fluids. If you have oral sex, you should be using condoms and vaginal condoms as well. Know your numbers. If you are having sex, it's important to get tested for STIs at least once a year, if you have multiple partners, try for at least every 6 months if you can. Safe sex is the only kind of sex to have. Diseases and pregnancy *can* happen to you. Don't be naïve, be diligent and be safe.

    Being in control of your sexual life and health is your right. You can do whatever and whoever you want to but when you look yourself in the mirror, how do you honestly feel about yourself? Are you proud of your actions deep down? If there ever comes a day that you are not proud of who you have become, you know what to do. You're worth so much more and you owe yourself the very best.

10

Love

"The best love is like a secret that everyone else has heard the rumor about, but only the two of you can confirm the full truth about."
-Shaleea Venney

You know that couple you follow on the gram because you admire them? We've all seen this couple. She's always posting pics of the flowers and jewelry he buys her for no reason at all. He posts pics of her as his "Woman crush everyday" and his "Bae" while traveling around the world. We see them and think "GOALS! Must be nice" or hashtag "Relationship goals". Newsflash, it isn't real. Each of these couples have been through hell and back at some point in their relationship. Don't look at their relationship and where it is now, and covet what they have. I guarantee you, they had to go through the struggle to end up in their "Happily ever after". You will not start a relationship and be on that level right away. That level takes time, tears, maturity, patience, forgiveness, and growth to achieve. There is no relationship that has put in real time, that hasn't seen it's fair share of hurt and drama. They may be smiling now, but I can assure you, they have cried together, broken up, lied, and hurt each other at some point in their relationship. Even your favorite couple has fights. Understand that real love takes work and commitment to each other.

  I'm not saying their relationship or love is not real, I'm saying that the perfect portrayal of love that people put out there is not always real. People are so set on appearing to have the perfect relationship that they post only half truths. She could be posting the jewelry he just bought her but what you don't know is, it was a gift he gave her for cheating on her. He may be posting pics of his "Bae" online but what you don't know is that he's a serial cheater. Don't let other people's takes on love influence your idea of what love looks like. Everybody's relationship is different and the worst thing you can do is compare your love to someone else's.

  I married the love of my life: that guy that knocked me up when I was 15, and we lived happily ever after. Well… We lived ever after, but it took a long time to get to the happily part. Many days we lived broke ever after, sadly ever after, broken ever after, and angry ever after. Our relationship and marriage has shown us all the best and worst parts of love. Since we have been together since we were kids, we have had the pleasure of watching each other grow up. He took much longer than me. He has lied and cheated on me more times than I care to admit to. He used to make me feel so unattractive because I couldn't understand why on earth he would need to cheat on me when I was such a good and beautiful woman. It really affected my self-esteem. It always seemed like the girls he would cheat on me with were everything I was not…in a bad way. I'm not saying it would've made me feel better if they were more attractive, but at least if they were more attractive, I wouldn't have felt so bad. I used to always tell him "You don't cheat down! If you're going to cheat at least let her be on my level. You're supposed to cheat up or what's the point". My goodness. Is there ever a "Right way" to feel about this? How could I have ever justified his actions? It shouldn't have happened in the first place! I cringe when I look back at that girl and the things she went through because she was in love.

We have had fights about money because I was always the more responsible one. He was always so carefree and could be outright careless when it came down to money. I always hated most of his friends because they were children walking around pretending to be men. I wanted him to have mature and responsible friends. He instead held onto most of his childhood friends. They suffered from arrested development and wanted to hang out and act the way they did when they were kids, but they were all grown men with children. They liked to drink and never had anything constructive going for them. It took him a long time to see why this was a problem in our relationship. The problem that he couldn't see was that he and his friends weren't on the same page. My husband was a grown man with a wife, a place, children, and bills to pay. His friends were mostly in between baby mamas, living with other people or their mothers, without jobs, real bills, or responsibilities. - No stability. Am I judging them? Not really. The fact of the matter is, I never really hated them as people, I hated their situations and choices. Truth of the matter is, none of them are bad people. The main difference between them and my husband is simple: my husband had a lot more to lose than any of his friends. His friends could chase girls, spend their money how they saw fit, go to jail for stupid reasons like being drunk in public, drink, smoke, or do whatever else they wanted to their heart's contentment. My husband could not. Every decision that my husband makes will affect all of us. He isn't living for himself anymore. He has 2 kids looking up to him who need food, shelter, and other basic-necessities. If anything happened to him or our union, it would be a lot of losing for all of us.

Never surround yourself with people who have less to lose than you do. When people don't have anything real going for themselves, it's very hard for them to comprehend your situation. Never ask for relationship advice from anyone who doesn't have a solid relationship. How can you advise me what to do in my marriage when you have never been married? I should listen to you about marital concerns, but I haven't seen you maintain one stable relationship? No, pass on that advice.

One day you will fall in love. It is my ultimate hope that you find someone to love and cherish you unconditionally. When you do find love, go in with your eyes open so that you are not disappointed. Love is hard and a full time job when you do it right. It's not always roses and candies. Sometimes it's curling up into a ball crying your eyes out. It's an argument because he interpreted what you said wrong or, because you couldn't read his mind when he needed something from you that he never told you about. Love is the most beautiful and ugliest thing in the world when it's real. Sometimes I hate my husband and can't figure out why I am still married to him. Moments later, I can't picture my life without him.

Don't compare your relationship with anyone else's. Their love story is not your love story. Their financial outlook may look differently than yours. If your guy can't afford grand gestures, that doesn't mean his love for you is any less than your friend's guy who can. Appreciate your partner for who he is and love him that way. Don't try to change him into your idea of what you think he should be. Love, real love, will make a man change on his own. There's something about real love and the right woman, that will cause a man to see the error in his ways and want to step up to be all that he can be for you. He will need to do that on his own. No matter how much you try to change him, it will never work. He will not change until he wants to. If a man refuses to change, he simply is not the right man for you. Count your losses and don't be afraid to move on. You don't have to put up with being treated badly. Don't ever talk down to your guy about his current state in life. If you know that he is trying, respect that. Where he is today, will not be where he is tomorrow. It is a process. Hang in there. No one is great right away. It takes time. Don't be against building with your guy.

Understand that love is not the fairy tale you see in the movies. Real love is not always grand and public. The best love is like a secret that everyone else has heard the rumor about, but only the two of you can confirm the full truth about. It fills your heart with butterflies and joy. You don't get tired of him. You could spend the whole day with him and miss him as soon as he leaves. You'll think about him all the time. He'll go out of his way to make you feel special, because you are. Never settle for a man who doesn't treat you as if he's lucky to have you.

First comes love, then comes marriage.

One day, he will ask you to marry him, and you will say yes. Enjoy your moment. Be engaged and in love. There's no need to rush into the marriage if you don't want to. Depending on how long you've known each other, have a longer engagement. Perhaps 1-2 years. If you've been together for some time already, it's ok to plan the wedding sooner. The main thing that matters is that you know the man you are marrying. People will try to scare you by saying that 50% of marriages end in divorce. That statistic is true but, realize that the number is probably as high as it is because most of these people had no business getting married in the first place. Marriage is not a game, or a joke. You don't get married just to say you have a husband or to have a wedding. Get to know that young man well before saying "I do". Pay special attention to the way he treats you, respects you, and loves you. Take bad habits seriously. Know your deal breakers. Knowing your deal breakers is crucial to your happiness. For example, cheating is a deal breaker. Smoking might be a deal breaker. As much as I love my husband, I understand now that you cannot fully love someone else until you first love yourself. Loving myself means setting standards in my relationship and honoring them so that I can be loved, protected, and respected. You must communicate with your guy so that you can have a clear understanding that works for the both of you.

You must pay attention to the signs. Trust your gut instinct. Chances are, your man is not going to change after you get married. If anything, marriage may make his habit/issue worse. Know where he stands financially. Is he a spender or a saver? Does he want children? How many? Do you? What are his thoughts on parenting? Does he go to church? Do you? Is it a deal breaker if he doesn't worship the way you do? What are his political views? Is he selfish? What are his plans? Does he have a plan for your future? Are there things that he thinks are ok, but are hard limits for you? What are those? Drinking? Smoking? You need to ask yourself some tough questions. If you are not honest with yourself, the honeymoon period will wear off and you'll find yourself knee deep in a marriage with someone you don't know or like. Take your time.

Don't let anyone rush you into getting married. Get married when the both of you feel like it's the right time. We didn't get married right away. I always knew I wanted to marry him, I loved him. I knew that when I married him, I didn't want to get divorced. If we had gotten married when our parents and family wanted us to, we'd probably be divorced right now. We'd already had two children and were very much together. He was still very immature and I knew it. I'd been wearing a ring that he had given me since I was 16. We got married when I was 22 and he was 25. It sounds backwards, but I told him that I wouldn't move into our own place until we were married. We got our first place and were supposed to get married on Friday and move in on Saturday. We ended up moving in on Friday and getting married on Saturday.

We didn't have a big grand wedding either. We were married in his aunts living room by his grandfather who raised him and was a preacher. We both wore jeans and t-shirts and our kids watched. His grandfather wasn't in the best health anymore and was home bound. The family questioned whether he'd even be able to marry us. He did.

He ministered to us about life, marriage, and staying together no matter what trial or tribulation came our way. His grandparents had been married 65 years before she died the year before. It was so special and beautiful. He told us how they were married under a tree in a backyard. He blessed us so much that day and it meant everything to my husband to have his hero marry us. When he died a few months after that, the magnitude of his final gift to us resonated even more. I wouldn't trade our wedding day for anything. It was perfect.

I tell you this to tell you that it doesn't matter if you have a big grand ceremony. The only thing that matters is that you both show up. You don't need 300 guests to declare your love to one another. I have seen people go into debt trying to keep up with the Joneses. I have seen people have big beautiful weddings and announce their divorce soon after. The whole thing was more of a show than the union of two souls. I'd rather you spend that huge sum of money on your down payment for your first home, or to go and see the world. It's nothing wrong with wanting to have a nice wedding but be practical. Do you really need all of that, or are you trying to impress people by having an over the top wedding? Your wedding is not for them, it's for you. I'm not downing anyone who had an extremely expensive wedding if they can afford it but, don't get into crazy debt trying to get married. All I'm saying is focus on the marriage and not the wedding. The wedding is one day but the marriage is supposed to be forever. Worry about the things that matter, like the commitment you are making to one another and the Lord, or pre-marital counseling so you can be better prepared for marriage. Love is beautiful. Marriage is supposed to be sacred. Honor your union, be a great wife, partner, and friend. Love him with all your heart, pray, and keep God in the center of your marriage and you will be just fine.

11

Peer Pressure (The "In" Crowd)

"Be comfortable enough in your own skin to not care what other people think of you. Find your crowd and be in with them."
-Shaleea Venney

So, you want to popular huh? It's ok to admit it. Here's the better question: *Why* do you want to be popular? So that everyone knows your name? It's cool to fit in with the "In crowd?" The popular people have it easier? So that others will be jealous of you? So that you won't feel like such an outcast?

Popular people are often seen as attractive and outgoing. Everyone wants to be their friends and they seem so perfect…looking in from the outside. The most important thing to remember about popularity is to be yourself.

I'd rather you have a small group of friends who are just like you and be genuinely well liked, than to be deemed popular by a group of friends who are nothing like you. You'd be forced to work hard everyday, trying to be more like them so that you can continue to fit in. Trying to be something you're not is a lot of work.

You need to find your clique. There's nothing wrong with wanting to make friends but it would serve you well to make friends with like minded people. If you are the band geek, make friends with the other band geeks. If you are the jock, other jocks will probably be your friends. Cheerleaders usually hang out with the other cheerleaders. Find your crew and stick with them. This will save you so much unnecessary heartache.

If you are not the confident outgoing type and a serious student, why would you want to start picking up friends who are ditching classes and failing? You take school seriously, they don't. What do you have in common? Am I saying that you need to live a life where you can only be friends with like minded people? Of course not. There's a quote I like: Pick your friends like you pick your fruit. I wouldn't choose the rotten apples, or the fruit that looks dented because they wouldn't be any good to me. What I am saying is that if you are not careful when choosing your friends, you might end up in some unsavory situations.

Some people mentally develop later than others. Let's say you're very immature and a big kid at heart. You start hanging with the "In crowd". They are wearing makeup, smoking cigarettes, drinking alcohol, and having sex. All these things are completely foreign to you and you wouldn't think of doing any of them on your own. Your new friends like you and you like the fact that they like you. The next time they pass around the alcohol bottle, cigarette, or illicit drug, perhaps you try it. You wouldn't want them to see you not being cool would you?

Now your clothes are tighter, you're talking differently, and you're a totally different person. You're not *you* anymore, you're…them. The truth is, they don't really like you. They like themselves. They like you for who they've turned you into. Here's how you can tell if your friends are really into you. Did you have to change who you were to be around them? Can you be your true self around them and they'd still hang with you? Would you be embarrassed to tell them about your favorite hobbies? Do you have a friend who only likes you when their other friends aren't around? If you tell them a secret, will they keep it? If you don't like the answer to any of these questions, you are dealing with fake friends.

If they talk about one of your friends behind their back when they're with you and pretend to be best friends with the person when they come around, the truth is, they talk about you behind your back when you're not around too. You need to be able to recognize the signs because if you cannot, you will let people who don't even mean you well, affect the way that you see yourself. What they think of you could really affect your self-esteem. Is it worth it? Your friendships won't even last.

The "In crowd" is dangerous. It is real work to get in with them and it's even harder to remain popular once you do. They can put a lot of pressure on you to be what they deem as cool and the cool threshold often changes week to week. Understand that this does not apply to all people in the "In crowd" but it does apply to a lot of them. Lots of the people in the "In crowd" drink, smoke, or use drugs sometimes because they think these things make them cool. Drinking is dangerous and can lead to alcohol poisoning and serious impairment of your mental and physical abilities. Smoking and secondhand smoking, are dangerous and could lead to a lifetime of addiction and pulmonary disease. Drugs are all bad and there's no such thing as a harmless drug. I've had more people than I can count remind me of how marijuana comes from the earth all while buying it from dispensaries that have laced it with all sorts of chemicals that we aren't sure what lasting effects they cause on the body yet. Yes, weed does come from the earth, but I have seen some very unproductive people who smoke it and are extremely addicted to it. Now, is every weed smoker a bum and loser? Of course not but, it's better to not even go there. This new generation loves to pop pills, and sip lean. Some think that because it's prescribed by a doctor it's safe. These pills are extremely addictive and if you are not in any actual pain, you should not be taking them. Their addicting effects are no joke and they're hard habits to break. You could be spending your time and money much more wisely than doing drugs, smoking, or drinking. Your health will thank you later.

Be comfortable enough in your own skin to not care what other people think of you. Find your crowd and be in with them. Don't try and hang with people who are nothing like you. When you hang with people who have similar interests and mindsets, you won't have to fake being someone you're not trying to impress them. Plus, you're more likely to find genuine friends when you stick with your tribe.

Justin Timberlake, Selena Gomez, Steven Spielberg, Rihanna, Chris Rock, and Barack Obama have admitted that they weren't cool in school, were bullied, or both. Bet those mean people are kicking themselves now. Moral of the story, you never know who someone will grow up to be. Lots of people who are cool in school will only be cool in school. Those years are sometimes the best of their lives. They were so popular and respected in school that we thought they'd always be on top of the world. Some of the people I wanted to be friends with, or that bullied me in school, didn't become very successful. I've run into many of them working as cashiers at fast food places, Walmart's, or pulling out public assistance cards to pay for their items. This is not to shame them. I'm sure they work hard, the point is, what others think of you doesn't determine your destiny. You never know who someone may turn out to be. The same people that you think are on top of the world now, might be singing a different tune later. The people they make fun of for being uncool, are often the people who go on to change the world and become millionaires.

Don't be anxious to fit in. Just walk in confidence, be your best self, and be kind to everyone. When you like you, others will also like you and they will gravitate towards your authenticity. You won't need to go for looking for the "In crowd", you will be the "In crowd" and without compromising any of your integrity or beliefs. That sounds like a win.

12

Don't Be in Such A Rush To Grow Up/You Can't Get Your Youth Back!

> "You're a kid for only a few years and then you're an adult for the rest of your life."
> -Shaleea Venney

There is a meme circulating around the internet that makes me laugh and makes me sad at the same time because it's so true. The meme depicts a 13 year old girls' picture from about 10-15 years ago on the left, and a 13 year old girls' picture from present day on the right. The girl on the left is wearing loose fitting jean shorts, a mickey mouse t-shirt, mickey mouse ears, and tennis shoes. She looks happy and innocent. The girl on the right is wearing red lipstick, a full face of makeup, short and tight ripped jean shorts, a crop top, and gladiator sandals. She is staring at the camera, poking her lips out, and striking the sexist pose she can (think butt poked out, right hand grabbing a handful of hair, and left hand on her hip). I would guess that she was much older than she was if someone asked me and I didn't already know her age.

Today's society is all about looking as sexy as possible and growing up as fast as possible. No one plays outside anymore. Your generation will never know the joy of red light green light, freeze tag, or Tag! You're it. Water balloon fights were the best part of hot days. If I had a dollar for every time we got in trouble for not being in the house when the street lights came on, I'd be wealthy.

There was a yearning for independence and to grow up back then just like there's a yearning for independence right now but in very different ways. Back in the day, our independence meant, we'd get summer jobs, learn to drive, and have a full list of household responsibilities. We weren't allowed to sit at home all day and do nothing. Our parents would've told us to go outside or find something to do. It forced us to use our ingenuity and think outside the box. Present day independence looks like asking for a phone and downloading apps so you can be more social with people on a device than you are in person. It looks like not pitching in at home around the house as much as you should, not really learning how to do much of anything for yourselves, wanting everything handed to you, and being too lazy to look something up with a quick google search. Do you understand that we didn't have google? We had to look up everything we wanted to know and find answers in books. There was a time when google didn't exist. Just wanted you to know!

The "Every person on the team gets a trophy" mentality of this generation paired with the need to grow up quickly and mimic what you see grown people doing, can lead to a dangerous combination. There is a self-aggrandizing, narcissistic, blind leading the blind, emotional unavailability that terrifies me. Work ethic is dying, and you want everything right now instantaneously. To make things worse, whenever the older people who have any kind of real life experience try to educate you, you dismiss them because you think you know everything already.

You don't.

Then there's the problem that you're developing faster than ever before too. The world is full of little girls in fully grown women sized bodies. Your breasts grow faster than your brains. The fact that you are fully developed doesn't give you the license to do whatever you want. Your body may have matured but you are mentally and emotionally immature. Let life come to you and happen when it's supposed to. Stop rushing to make things happen. When children rush to enter an adult world, they lose their innocence at a high price and your innocence can never be returned to you once you lose it.

Balance is so important. Create a balance if you can. Enjoy your youth and have fun. Being mature and being "fast" are two different things. Mature people have their own minds and are not easily swayed by what everyone else is doing. Mature people are able to make their own decisions without fear of judgment. They are secure in themselves. Fast girls are all about the attention and the likes. They dress provocatively and live faster than they should. They are easily manipulated. They are insecure and too blind to even realize their own truths. Maturity is knowing that all of our actions good or bad- have consequences.

Be a kid for as long as you can. Enjoy not having any real responsibilities. You're a kid for only a few years and then you're an adult for the rest of your life. Think about it, you're born, you're five, then turn ten. A few years later, you're no longer a kid, you're thirteen. Next thing you know, sixteen rolls around and you can start driving. Before you know it, it's prom, you reach 18, graduate, and it's off to college or into the workforce. You've made it to adulthood. You're going to live in adulthood for the rest of your days now. 20s, 30s, 40s, 50s, 60s, and so on. You're an adult so much longer than you're a kid. There is no need to rush, you'll be an adult soon enough. Smell the Play-doh, play with toys, laugh, go to amusement parks, and play games. Do as much as you can while you can. Adulthood brings its own set of life issues. Bills, rents/mortgage, jobs, children, etc. One day you will look back and miss the very things you hate about being young right now. I promise you. It goes by fast, don't speed up the process.

13

Role Models/ What Are You Seeing?

"We don't need another beautiful naked woman on social media, we need women who are ready to evoke change in the world."
-Shaleea Venney

Where I come from, the streets weren't lined with successful polished women. I didn't see very many successful women that looked like me in my family either. It can be very hard to desire or reach for things that you cannot see. If you never try something, how will you know whether you love or hate it? If you're not surrounded by positive, or successful people, it can be hard to imagine becoming one. If your situation sounds anything like mine, it's very important that you cultivate some semblance of what success looks like to you.

Understand that no matter where you come from or what you've seen, you can be anything you want to be. No matter who your parents are or how high the odds are stacked against you, you can become a success if you want to become a success. You will have to work for it but, it can be done.

ROLE MODELS/ WHAT ARE YOU SEEING?

I suggest you choose a role model. Your role model could be a teacher, a parent, a friend of the family, a family member, or even someone you see on TV. You don't have to know someone personally. You can look up to her from afar. Choose a woman who exemplifies what your idea of success and happiness looks like. It's important to start trying to figure out what kind of life you want to have. Do you want to be the boss, the employee, the creative, or the free spirit? Do you work 40 hours a week in an office, or do you travel for work? Maybe you work from home. What are you good at? What do you see yourself becoming one day? What sort of schooling does it take to get there? Find someone who is already doing it. Study them. How did they get to where they are today? Are you willing to work as hard as they did? It's never too early or too late to have someone inspire you but you're going to need to put the work in.

Find a woman with some substance I beg you. Female bosses are my favorite! When I say substance, I simply mean, a woman who stands for something. An educated woman. A real go-getter. A woman with morale and an honor system. I know this is hard because so many look up to "Famous because they're famous" people but, I want you to add value to this world. We don't need another beautiful naked woman on social media, we need women who are ready to evoke change in the world. We need women who can be the CEO of the next game changing company. We need the woman who can successfully run for president and win. We need more Oprah's and scientists. I want you to be so successful that you never have to look for a seat at anyone else's table because you've built your own.

I found my role model on accident. My parents were huge Cosby Show fans, so we'd have to watch it with them. On the show, the mother, Claire Huxtable played by the amazing Phylicia Rashad, was the woman I wanted to be. From the first time I saw her, I was so intrigued that I found myself watching all the time. She was classy, educated (a lawyer), had a loving husband, was beautiful, dressed sharply, and always seemed to have it all together. As soon as I saw her, I wanted to be her. I had never seen such beauty and grace on the tv before. In fact, it is because of Claire Huxtable, that my younger self wanted to become a lawyer. To this day, I still adore Phylicia Rashad because I learned that she is just as much of a class act off screen as she is on. Another role model I have today, is without a doubt Michelle Obama. The fact that she is a lawyer too is merely a coincidence.

Who inspires you that much? Who do you secretly want to be like? Pay attention to her and learn everything you can from her. Do your research. Learn how she got started, what setbacks she had to face, and how she made it. While I want you to draw your inspiration from her, remember that she is the only her there is, you must be yourself. Don't try to be her because you weren't meant to walk in her shoes, you were meant to walk in your own. Ask questions if you can. Take notes. Don't be shy or too reserved. Your dreams need to make you excited and awaken your inner courage. Be bold and fearless in the pursuit of your dreams.

The admiration you develop for your role model will be essential to your life's path because your admiration will grow into respect. Respect is the most important part of the equation because, respect will grow into action. It is very hard to watch a successful person and not be inspired to get up and go towards your own dreams. Successful people should serve as a constant reminder that if they made it, your dream is not impossible to attain, it just needs determination and focus. Never be jealous of successful people. Be inspired, be motivated.

You can always make minor tweaks to your role model as you learn and progress to your next chapters. This is normal. Your vision today will change tomorrow. Change is constant and necessary.

At each stage of your journey, choose your role model carefully. Choose a role model that can meet you where you are currently but also speaks to the woman that you'd like to become. Always remember that one day you will be someone's role model too and when that day comes, remember your humble beginnings and pay it forward.

14

Education

"Everybody has their own unique something to bring to the table. Pull up a chair and devour each lesson."
-Shaleea Venney

It may sound like a cliché but, stay in school. Learn as much as you can. There are successful people who didn't go to college and it is possible to accrue lots of student loan debt in your pursuit of a degree. I understand both of those points because they are valid. Nonetheless, understand that your education is important. Your education is one of the only things that no one can ever take away from you. I don't want you to get an education to make money (sure money will come), I want you to get an education so that you can learn to think. You could hit the lottery tomorrow and I would still press for you to obtain an education. English Poet and Author Thomas Tusser once famously said: "A fool and his money will soon be parted". Simply put, if you come into a cash windfall and are not educated enough to handle it, you will blow it quickly on depreciating assets and be broke again in no time because you are not financially literate. Educate yourself.

When you decide what you want to become professionally, educate yourself about that line of work. When you find a concept that you feel ignites a fire inside of you, educate yourself. There are plenty of nontraditional ways to educate yourself. Learn all you can about the topic that interests you. Never stop learning. You're never going to be too old to learn something new. Don't ever be the person who thinks they know everything and isn't open to learning something new. There will always be something new that you can learn. Be open. You will never be too educated.

Read often. I can't stress enough the need to be well read. Read books from people that don't think like you or come from the same place as you. You know how you think, listen to someone else's opinion so that you can gain more insight. It's never a bad idea to immerse yourself in an idea or culture that differs from your own. The world is full of beautiful people and opportunities to learn from. Everybody has their own unique something to bring to the table. Pull up a chair and devour each lesson.

Learning doesn't always need to take place in a classroom. Life experiences are great educators. Hands on work can teach you a ton about the field you choose and about yourself. Don't be afraid to roll up your sleeves and do the work. I've always been a firm believer that school teaches us the basics and it is up to us to continue our educational journeys on our own.

Write often too. Studies have shown that writing things down helps you to remember them better. Write down your thoughts and memories. Keep a journal. Write down whatever you fear, love, and hope for. Document your dreams and favorite quotes. Just something for your future self, from your younger self. Writing down your thoughts is a great therapeutic tool to combat stress.

While education is the key to success, it's not the only key there is.

Some people have unlocked their potential with different keys, but an education is a solid foundation. When you decide what you want to be, decide carefully. Choose your major, career, and even college/university carefully. Try and get as many scholarships as you can. Decide what works best for you and your family financially. Look in to applying for grants. Perhaps you can play a sport or an instrument to offset some of the costs of college. Earn a degree that you're passionate about but that is also in demand and will allow you to earn a good living.

Your education must be taken seriously and be pursued with focus and determination. It is a huge part of the foundation that the rest of your life will be built upon. See that book? Crack it open.

15

Set Future Goals

"Don't be haunted by the regrets of not walking in your purpose."
-Shaleea Venney

Plan for your future. Even if it doesn't work out the way you plan, plan anyway. You must plan on being successful. It doesn't just happen, it needs to be intentional. There is a quote by Antoine de Saint-Exupery I love that reads: "A goal without a plan is only a wish." So true.

Once you create your goals, you must create a plan for how you will see your goal through to fruition. If your goal is to get into college, you need to be preparing throughout high school. Plan on doing your homework, joining clubs, studying, and applying yourself so that you can maintain the best GPA you possibly can. If you want to sing or act, you need to perfect your craft. Voice lessons, acting lessons, and head shots will be needed. If you want to be a Veterinarian and work with animals one day, perhaps you could try volunteering at local shelters or animal hospitals to start preparing. Whatever your goal is, you need to set a plan in place to achieve it. No dream can come to pass without careful planning and putting in the work. The most important part of a plan is that it is supposed to be measurable. You must be careful not to fall into the trap of saying "I will do this" or "I plan on doing that" WHEN?! Setting a goal is the *I will* part but, the measurable plan part is all about the date you circle on the calendar. Your thought process should sound more like: "I will do this by the end of the summer, or by December 1st". Give yourself a schedule and a time frame to achieve your goals so that you can check little tasks off the list and be encouraged to keep going. A goal is really just a group of little tasks that must be checked off to achieve the bigger picture.

Don't ever be the kind of person who is always talking about what you're going to do, but never makes any effort. Everyone knows that person who is full of potential and could be anything they want to be but aren't much, because they're lazy. They're always declaring every New Year's Eve that "This is going to be my year" or telling you about their visions and plans only to have another year roll by that they remained stagnant in their situation. Just try. Just start.

Dream! Dream as big as you can. Never let anyone tell you what or who you can be or what you're capable of. If you have a dream or a vision inside of you, you go for it with everything you've got. The main people telling you why it won't work are the same people who let their own dreams die. They don't have anything going on for themselves, so they will try to crush your dreams so that you can remain as low as they are. Everybody is not supposed to see your vision. It's ok. Asking other people to see your vision is like wearing a VR headset and expecting other people to experience the twists and turns with you. They can't. They can see you jumping and going through the adventure and even think it's cool, but they can't see it for themselves. Whatever is in your heart is meant to be there. Listen to your instincts and work to bring it to a tangible reality. The best way to show people what's in you, is to show them what's in you. Naysayers will soon be converted to believers.

SET FUTURE GOALS

My Pastor Fred Price Jr. of Crenshaw Christian Center LA, once told me that my purpose is tied to my passion. He told me that while I may be good at doing whatever I set my mind to, I would never be happy until I pursue my passion and my gifts. He was right. The thing that you love doing the most, the thing that comes naturally to you that you wish you could spend all your time doing. Could you do it for free and be happy? That is your passion. You were created to do that exact thing. Figure out how to use your passion to create revenue so that you can provide for yourself and you will live your best life. Don't worry about how to make it happen. Proverbs 18:16 in the bible says that: Your gift will make room for you and bring you into the presence of great people. That simply means, when you are gifted, doors will open that you never thought would open and great people will be drawn to you. You won't have to chase them . Just do your work and they'll find you. Success is coming, it's only a matter of time.

I became a nurse because I was already working in the medical field and becoming a nurse just seemed like the next step in career advancement. I've always excelled in school and knew that I could become a nurse if I tried. Plain and simple. Do I like being a nurse? Sure. I love the patients and helping them. Would I quit my nursing job tomorrow if I could write and speak full time? In a heartbeat. Sometimes I experience tons of heartache and sadness because in my gut, somewhere deep down in my soul, there is a longing to be more. It's like deep down, my soul knows I was never meant to be doing what I am doing. There were so many days I would be driving to work crying my eyes out, out of sheer despair. I have been thankful for my career don't get me wrong, but I know there is more to life. I know who I am supposed to be. I have always known, I just lost my way for a little while. When I told people I wanted to be a writer, they told me I'd never make a good living that way. I believed them more than I believed in myself. That's why it's important for you to set a plan in motion to achieve whatever dream you have inside of you. If you don't at least give it an effort, you will always have regrets and wonder "What if" even if you are successful doing something else. You might as well go for what you really love out of the gate, because if you don't, it will continue to take a huge toll on your life either way. You'll smile and hide your truth from the world, but you'll never keep it from yourself. Don't be haunted by the regrets of not walking in your purpose.

I must say this to you as well: If you love something and feel it's what you want to do, go for it. Don't let anyone push their idea of who you should be on to you. If you don't want to be a lawyer, doctor, or have a "Big time" job, if you want to bake cakes, fix cars, or do hair. Even if your idea of success doesn't involve a board room or a 4 year degree, go after it. You should be doing whatever it is that you are passionate about. Some of the most traditionally "Successful" people aren't truly happy. I know doctors who hate their jobs and are only doctors because their parents wanted them to be. No one can live your life for you or through you. If you want to fix cars, fix cars. Everyone doesn't want to be the CEO. Some people want to be artists, or butchers. Don't let anyone make you feel bad about who or what you want to be. Of course, I want you to struggle as little as possible-hence the setting goals and planning part but, your idea of success might look differently than mine or hers. At the end of the day, do you like it? Congratulations! You are successful.

Today, no matter where you are on your journey, ask yourself one question: What do I want? What do you want? What will make you happy? What kind of desire is burning inside of you? Write that down. That is your goal. Now, think about what it will take to get there and give yourself a time frame. Write that down too. That is your plan. I've given you step one and two, but the focus and determination are yours alone.

16

Depression

> "It's not your responsibility to keep their secret, it's your responsibility to save their life."
> -Shaleea Venney

I realize that your struggle to like yourself and smile may be impossible at times. You might be smiling on the surface but dealing with an inner turmoil so severe, that you are battling depression. Mental illness is not a topic that we can afford to take lightly. We must take it seriously.

First, I'd like to start by giving you permission to be depressed. Your feelings are valid even if no one else sees them. No one gets to tell you how you feel, because they are not the ones living with what you are living with.

Because I understand that the pain you are feeling is real, I urge you to not go at it alone. You need to tell someone what you are dealing with. You *do* have family and friends who care about you. Sometimes people get so caught up with their own issues, that they miss your silent cries for help. I apologize on their behalf. Just because people haven't noticed what you are dealing with, doesn't mean that they don't care. Allow yourself to be vulnerable enough to share your heart with someone you trust. You might be surprised how much people will rally around you when they know how much you've been hurting.

Your family, school, boyfriend, sexuality, childhood trauma, loss of a loved one, bully, or anything else you can think of. NONE of these things are a valid reason to feel like you have no other options. Sometimes we get depressed for a specific reason like one of those stated above. This situational depression won't last forever. There is always a way out. Don't let your current situation make you believe that things can never get better. Whatever you are dealing with will eventually be over. You will eventually be able to get out of that school, house, relationship, or memory. It won't always be bad times. Don't give up because you can't see the light at the end of the tunnel right now, it is there. Hold on. Right now you are looking at everything that you have already been through but, don't allow your painful past to rob you of the beautiful future that is to come. Your current circumstances are not a reflection of where you are destined to go.

Find what makes you happy. Whatever it is you love doing, do more of that. If anyone makes you happy, spend more time with that person. Find every opportunity you can to escape whatever is holding your thoughts prisoner. What are you doing when you are the happiest? If you are so severely depressed that nothing makes you happy, please seek help immediately. If you ever find yourself so low that you can see no way out, fight! You must fight to find the strength to seek help. In my community, we pray about everything. Prayer is great but, seeking help doesn't mean you don't trust God to help you. Seeking help doesn't make you weak or soft, it makes you strong and brave. Many people die because they keep it to themselves. Tell someone. Teacher, boss, friend, sibling, neighbor, parent. Anyone. Dial the suicide hotline 800-273-8255. You must do whatever you can to get the support you need. Please don't give up on yourself. You matter. You are beautiful. You are special. The world would miss you if you left it.

If you have never battled depression for yourself, it is your job to be a diligent friend and resource for those who do. With the high numbers of people battling depression these days, it is highly likely that someone you know is currently secretly dealing with depression. It is very important for you to recognize the signs so that you can be their beacon of hope to help them through it.

You'd probably think that you should be concerned for the quiet, sad, introverted girl or guy. This is true, you should pay attention to them and seek help for them if you feel they need it. The person I want to especially address is the one who has everything together by all appearances. They always seem happy, they're always going. They juggle so many responsibilities, they wear many different hats. They are the person everyone calls when times are hard. That is the person you need to watch out for. People like this are so busy taking care of everyone else, that they often neglect their own mental and physical needs and when they're overwhelmed and mentally exhausted, they often have no one to call. When you see someone acting like nothing ever bothers them and letting nothing get to them, that is a red flag. They need for you to see them because they will never tell you. The people that we see as the strongest, carry the heaviest loads. It can take a toll on even the strongest person. Depression is not a sign of weakness, it's a sign of being overwhelmed and not always being able to cope effectively. It's being human. How many times have you seen or heard of someone taking their life and those closest to them say something like "I never would've thought" or "She was always so happy" or "I just talked to her and she was fine". Pay attention. You never know what someone else might be struggling with in private.

You need to recognize the signs. One of the signs to look out for is mood swings. One minute they're up and the next they are down. They may talk about being a burden to others. Are they doing things out of the norm like drinking excessively or doing drugs? Acting recklessly is another red flag. When someone doesn't care if they live or die, be concerned. They may start sleeping too much or too little. They may start feeling hopeless, or voice that their life doesn't matter. Anxiety ensues. They may start isolating themselves from friends and family and not want to be bothered. The depressed person might start giving away their prized possessions without reason. Sometimes a person may tell you that they want to take their own life. Don't take this lightly if they share this with you. This is sometimes their way of asking for help. Ask them if they have a plan on how they will do it. If they have a plan, get them help right away but, seek help for them even if they don't have a plan. If you notice any of the above warning signs, see them as red flags and get help for your loved one. Don't wait, and do not keep what they have shared with you a secret. It's not your responsibility to keep their secret, it's your responsibility to save their life.

    Let's not let mental illness be the end of us or anyone we care for. Not one more life. Not on my watch. Not on your watch. Not on our watch!

17

Bullying

"You're either the bully or the bullied. Either way, I feel sorry for you."
-Shaleea Venney

While growing up, you will deal with your fair share of bullies. People are mean and have always been that way. Due to the safety people find in high tech anonymity, they are crueler and more scathing than before. Where do you fall in this situation? You're either the bully or the bullied. Either way, I feel sorry for you.

First, I want to address the bully. What comfort do you take in ruining someone else's day? Why are you so critical of other people? I have seen a great deal of bullying in my life and I have come to one conclusion: Happy people don't bully people, hurt people do. There is a pain inside of you that you haven't yet come to terms with. You unleash the aggression you have bottled up, on unsuspecting strangers whom you see as "Weak". There's many reasons you might be doing this. You might be stressed about things you have going on at home. Maybe your parents have split up or are tough disciplinarians. You might be lonely and bully other people because you think it makes you cool or will earn you some respect. Maybe there was a time when someone once bullied you and, you're now in a different city or town and made the decision that you would become the bully so that no one would bully you again. You generally don't feel very well liked, so you take it out on others. Maybe you just think it's funny to pick on people, and enjoy getting a rise out of others. None of these scenarios make it right and none of them make you unaccountable for your actions. Your pain doesn't give you a pass to hurt others.

The bully is even sadder than the bullied person. The bully, secretly feels the hate that they project on others for themselves. Your bullying is a cry for help. Getting laughs and tormenting other people is no way to gain respect. People tend to leave you alone and are nice to you out of fear because you're a bully, not because they respect you. No one really respects a bully. The average person cringes at your rudeness but is too afraid to speak up out of fear that you may turn on them too. If your idea of a good time involves tearing down the next person, you must ask yourself why. If the person you're bullying is so unimportant, why do you go out of your way to make their life hell each day? Do you ever think about what that must feel like for them? Picture that being your brother, sister, friend, or someone you care about. How would it make you feel seeing someone you cared for being harassed? The person you're harassing is also someone that is cared for. They are a brother, sister, friend, or loved one.

If you are the bullied, I want you to know that you are stronger than you think. First and foremost, recognize that you are not the weak pathetic person your bully is making you out to be. Understand that bullies often pick on you because they're jealous of something about you. Maybe you have beautiful hair, that she wishes she had. Perhaps the guy she likes, is interested in you. She might be jealous of parts of your body that she wishes she had. She could be jealous of your clothes, or your intelligence. Think about the thing that she makes fun of about you the most, that is what she secretly admires the most. No matter what she says to you, you must never subscribe to the lies she wants you to believe about yourself. Once you understand that the bullying is never about you and more about someone else's insecurities and issues, it's a lot easier to deal.

 Don't be timid and cower. If you are not one who wants to involve anyone in your conflict out of fear of what your bully will do, you must be brave enough to face him or her head on. My elders used to say "Stand up to your bully and they will never bother you again". I found this to be true. Bullies love the idea that you are afraid and that you won't fight back. In fact, they are counting on it. I am not telling you to go and get into a fight or do something foolish to your bully. I don't want you to go looking for trouble. If the bullying persists, and you find yourself backed up in a corner, you must not back down. Don't be afraid. Take a stand once and for all within reason of course. Never approach someone with a weapon of any sort. If you need to raise your voice, poke your chest out, and stand tall. Do it! Let them know you will not continue to take this. If the bully doesn't back down and picks a fight, you must defend yourself but, only if they start it. One of two things will happen, you might win the battle and surprise everyone including yourself, or you might get beat up. Either way this is a win. Even if you get beat up, the bully will recognize that you mean business and you will gain confidence in yourself. You'll be so proud of the day that you stood up for yourself. You will never forget it. Your bully won't either.

 When I was in school, I had bullies. Some didn't like my hair, others thought I talked too properly, still, others said I thought I was better than them. I learned that that was code for THEY thought I was better than them and hated me for it instead of trying to be my friend. I had Pepsi soda thrown into my hair for "Thinking I was cute". I was held down in a bathroom stall and had my breasts groped in the 9th grade by Junior class cheerleaders because they were sure I was stuffing my bra. I was followed from class to class once because a girl's boyfriend thought I was cute and she was not ok with it. I never even talked to the guy and in her mind, it was my fault that he thought I was cute. She wasn't mad at him but, at me for trying to dress cute. The best part of the story? We wore uniforms to school, so we were all dressed pretty much the same. I internalized what they said was wrong with me for a long time and didn't want to go to school just so I could avoid them. Running away from your problems is never going to solve them and I learned that the hard way. I had to face them. I stood up to them one day and tried to fight the biggest girl. I was in a rage fit and came across loud and clear. The girl backed down and they all looked at me, told me I needed to "Chill, it's not that serious" and walked away. They didn't bother me anymore after that day.

This day and age, people can bully you in person and online so it's like it never stops. It's understandable how a person can go crazy. Do whatever you need to do to be ok. Log off, take a break from social media, block the person, report their posts, unfollow them, don't look at their posts, make your page private, or anything else you can do. Don't allow anyone to harass you. Don't allow anyone to steal your joy and peace.

Bullying is never a good idea. It hurts everyone involved and no good can come from it. If you are friends with someone whom you know is a bully, speak up. Don't be afraid to go against the crowd. Maybe they continue to act the way they do because they see you laughing and feel empowered. We must speak up for others. If you are the bully, change your ways. What is fun and games to you may be a real hell for the person you are demonizing. You never know what someone else may be going through. Don't make a tough situation tougher by being a bully. Heaven forbid the person takes their own life. You would be responsible you know? If you are the bullied, remember that things won't always be this way. Get some help. Be brave, be strong, and hang in there. It will all work out.

18

Molestation

"Don't let the monster who hurt you succeed in taking your youth and your future."
-Shaleea Venney

If I will help you grow, I must be authentic and raw. My deepest truth... I was molested growing up. Not many people know about it to this day. It's hard for me to talk about it but I know that it is necessary if this is something that hits home for you. I will say it again, I was molested growing up. Deep cleansing exhale.

It was someone close to me. The first time I can remember was when I was 5 and my molester touched me on my private area. I was too young to understand what had happened but, old enough to know that whatever it was didn't feel right. This was the first time but not the last. It went on for years, the touching and groping. I didn't know what to do or who to tell. I was afraid. Finally, when enough was enough, I told my mother. She stared at me, her eyes wide, and said "Yeah right, I know that's not going on, and if it is, you are more than a victim. You never came to me before. You didn't try to stop it sooner. Girl, get out of here with this mess, I bet it won't happen again". My eyes puddled up and I went and sat in the bathroom, the only place in the house I could be alone, and cried my eyes out. I was really hurt but that conversation helped me to find the strength to fight back. I knew no one was going to help me, so I had to help myself.

One day, the molester, tried to take it a step further. I think I was 13 at the time. He attempted to pin me down and had every intention to rape me. There was no way I was going to lose my virginity in such a savage way. I mustered up all the strength in me and fought with everything I had. I was able to get him off me and grabbed a knife and cast-iron skillet. I waved them both at him and swore to God that I was ready to kill him where he stood if he came near me again. I meant it. I had every intent to stab him if he took one step closer to me. He backed down. My mother found out later and I wasn't apologetic. After that day, I began sleeping with a knife under my pillow. I didn't have any more instances after that, but the emotional damage remains even to this day.

The hardest part of being molested is when you're molested by someone close to you. I understand this well.

If you are someone who has been molested or is being molested or sexually abused, my heart goes out to you. I want you to know that it is not your fault. I want to apologize to you. Someone failed you. Someone didn't protect you. With all my heart, I sincerely apologize that this happened to you. It's incredibly hard to bear and it unfairly steals your innocence and trust.

If you are being molested right now, tell someone. If you're like me and that person doesn't help you or blames you, tell someone else. Tell someone until someone helps you out of the situation. Fight for yourself. When no one came to my rescue, I had to be my own hero. I hope this never happens to you but if it does, fight!

Forgive yourself. This goes for those currently in the situation and those who have been there in the past. Forgive yourself. It's easy to think about what you did wrong or what you could have done differently. Understand one thing, this should have never happened to you. You are the victim. Don't blame yourself. It's hard not to relive it, don't make things worse by blaming yourself.

Next, forgive the person who hurt you. The pain that you are carrying can easily evolve into depression, regret, bitterness, promiscuity, and stagnation. It is easy to get lost in the emotions. Forgiveness can free you of some of that. It's so hard to walk around carrying all of this on your shoulders. Being molested kills the little girl inside of you. Living in the aftermath kills any growth potential. Don't let the monster who hurt you succeed in taking your youth and your future. Forgive him for yourself. Forgive him for the future love of your life. Forgive him so that you can properly heal. You don't have to forget what happened to you, you just need to forgive the fact that it happened. If there is anyone who knew this was happening to you and didn't stop it, forgive them too. Heal your heart today. Drop the weight off your shoulders.

I have forgiven everyone involved in my situation. I would be lying if I told you it never crossed my mind. It's my own worst nightmare. It still haunts me sometimes. There is no magic fix it button but, it does get easier with time. Surround yourself with people who love and genuinely want nothing but the best for you and they will help you to a point of peace. Seek therapy, church, meditation, prayer, or whatever else you need to seek to make yourself whole, as long as it is constructive. You must come to terms with your pain and face it head on. Masking the pain with drugs, alcohol, men, or other vices will help temporarily but, will never solve the real problem, it must come from within.

I'm so sorry for what happened to you. I wish I could rewind the clock to a time before it happened and shield you from it. I want you to be safe. I want you to be free. I want to give you love, kind words, and hugs. Please know that you are above what happened to you and that you are worthy of better. You are stronger than what happened to you. You are courageous. You can be anyone you want to be. This trauma has nothing to do with how far you can go in life if you don't allow it to. You will always remember what happened to you, but you don't have to let it define you.

    Go and live your life sweetheart. This is only the beginning for you and your story is waiting to be beautifully written. You survived, and your attacker does not get to win.

19

Don't Ever Get Too Big To Pray!

"Growing up in my community, you learn to pray before you learn your ABC's."
-Shaleea Venney

Growing up in my community, you learn to pray before you learn your ABCs. Church and prayer are huge parts of everyday life. The problem is that some people tend to grow up and lose a bit of their relationship with God. It's not that people stop believing in God, it just seems like too many people reach a certain level of success, and leave the heavy praying back in their poorer days.

When we're in need of answered prayers, we go to church, pray, and talk to God constantly. We continue to pray until our prayer comes to pass and then, when we get out of the crisis, we don't talk to God until we find ourselves waist deep into the next one.

Talk to God. When times are good, when times are bad. Go to God. You must have a relationship with God. He must be a friend to you. When you have a good friend, you share your life with them. You talk about good times, you discuss bad times. You laugh together, you cry together. What happens when we neglect our friends? If a friend suddenly stopped talking to you without explanation, it would put a strain on your relationship. You would wonder why they didn't talk to you anymore and if there was something you may have done or said wrong. How would you feel if out of the blue, that friend suddenly called you only to ask you for a favor? They act like nothing has changed and you're on the same page you were on the last time you talked. Wouldn't that make you feel used? We've all had friends like that. The ones who only call us when they need something from us. You shouldn't be that sort of friend to anyone. You cannot be that kind of friend to God.

When you need direction in life, love, career moves, relationships, or finances, talk to God. If you work in retail or become President of the United States, talk to God. Don't ever get too far from God. Don't ever get so important or big that God isn't a factor in your life. You will never be bigger than God. Everything that you have been blessed with, is temporary and can be taken away from you. God is eternal and will never leave you.

Give thanks to God for everything He has brought you through. Give thanks to God for things you are praying for that He hasn't even done yet. It's so important to have a heart of gratitude and thanksgiving for God. Acknowledge Him in all your ways. Understand that nothing is possible without Him and that all things are possible through Him.

There is power in prayer. Prayer can be soulfully cleansing. Cry out to God. Mean your prayer with all your heart. Pray with sincerity. Be honest. Be authentic. There's nothing God doesn't know about you anyhow. You might as well be yourself.

You will lose your way and stumble sometimes. Life will not always go as planned. You will do things that are not pleasing to God. God knew everything you would ever do before you ever did it. He still loves you. There's not much you can do to make Him love you any less.

Forgive yourself, ask God for forgiveness and strive to be better. Do your best.

I have prayed my way through many storms. I am everything I am today and everything I will be in the future because of God. I take no credit. I am always seeking to be closer to Him. I talk to Him daily. I go to Him about everything that troubles me. If you want to know how I survived teen motherhood. God. How I knew I was supposed to be better than the situation I was in. God. How I went for my dreams. God. How I survived molestation. God. How I got out of the welfare line and back in school after dropping out. God. My marriage. God. My children. God. Do you see a pattern? By no strength of my own. I can take no credit. God did it all. Prayer and faith will change your life. It changed mine. There is much more evidence that suggests that God is real than there is that suggests that He isn't. The information is easily accessible if one seeks to find the answers. You must seek God for yourself and know Him for yourself. You cannot be saved and redeemed because your loved ones are. They can pray for you but your soul and relationship with Him, is ultimately your own responsibility.

If you are reading this and you are someone who doesn't know God or believe that He is real, remember this one thing: There is a 50% chance that you are correct and there is a 50% chance that I am correct. If I am wrong, then I'll have wasted my life trying to live as morally sound as possible doing what is right to the best of my ability. I'll have lived my life trying to help others and trying to spread positivity and light and when I die, I won't go to heaven or hell. If this is my potential legacy when I die, I am more than ok with it because I will have lived a meaningful life. Please understand, I am not saying that your disbelief that there is a God makes you a bad person, nor am I implying that you're not living a meaningful life. I am just concerned about your soul and eternity. I want you to experience God's love for yourself because it changes you for the better.

If I am right about God's existence, the above still applies but, my reward is that I get to spend forever and a day in heaven. I am willing to take this chance wholeheartedly. Are you? Are you willing to wager your eternity? You have a 50% chance of being correct, right?

God bless you.

20

Give Yourself Some Credit (Cards!)

"You never know you need credit until you find out you don't have any."
-Shaleea Venney

If there was one thing I could think of that I wish someone would've told me about growing up that they didn't, it would be to give myself some credit. Where I come from, people are not always financially responsible. People put bills in their kids' name's sometimes so needless to say, some parents don't have much to share with their children about how to be fiscally prepared. Most of us learned about credit the hard way. You never know you need credit until you find out you don't have any.

I am far from a credit expert, but I have good credit. I learned the hard way how much credit scores can affect your life. You want a nice place to live, want to buy or lease a car, eyeing that job, want a credit card? Credit matters in each of these scenarios. There are three credit bureaus. Experian, Transunion, and Equifax. They all judge you on different things so your 3 digit number may vary between the 3. I don't know the algorithm they use, but all these scores put together equate to what is called your Fico score. Your Fico score is brought to you by the Fair Issac Corporation and it is very important to know yours. Fico Scores range from a low 300 to a high 830.

You get grown and decide to get a credit card and you're approved. You max it out because you think it's free money and you're irresponsible. You never think about it again. This is going to haunt you. You must pay off your debt. You can't just abandon your responsibility if you ever hope to bounce back later and, you *will need* to bounce back later.

I learned about credit the hard way. I got credit cards early on, maxed them out, and didn't fully understand how the process worked. When I went to purchase my first car, I discovered that my credit was terrible and I couldn't get qualified to buy the car at a decent rate. The only banks willing to give me the loan, wanted to charge me outrageous interest rates. When you take out a loan, an interest rate is the portion of the loan that the bank charges you as the borrower. They are typically charged on an annual basis. The lousier your credit, the higher your interest rate. This will make your loan very expensive. This is the price you pay when your credit isn't good. There are lots of predatory lenders and financial institutions just waiting to take advantage of you because they know you're desperate. Some offer loans they know you won't be able to pay back reasonably. You might borrow $2000 and find yourself owing them $6000 or more sometimes. It's insane!

I learned that you have to take your credit journey into your own hands. I considered lots of credit repair companies that charged more than I could afford. These companies say "Hey, we know your credit is bad and we can help make it better…for a nominal fee". After some research, I decided to do it myself. I went online and filed disputes with each credit bureau asking them to remove some of the negative marks on my reports. Each credit bureau takes 30 days to do any updates and will email you with changes they have made, if any. It worked. They removed lots of stuff off my reports. Did you know that some of the negative items on your report might be in error? I didn't have to pay any credit repair company, I did it myself.

The next thing I researched was how to rebuild my credit. I downloaded the Credit Karma app on my phone so that I could see a good picture of my credit report and things I needed to work on going forward. Some people have talked down about the accuracy of Credit Karma but, I think it's a great free tool to learn how to improve your credit. Even if the scores aren't perfectly accurate, their free tools are an amazing resource to tell you where to start when you aren't sure what you're doing. They gave me tips. I learned it's a good idea to start out with a secured credit card when you're just starting out and your credit isn't good. The best option I found was the Capital One secured card. I applied for one of them and was immediately approved. Secured cards require you to put a deposit down to get them. For example, you put down $200 and when your card arrives, that will be your credit limit. The object of the game is to not use too much of your available credit or what the credit bureaus refer to as "Credit Utilization." Don't use your card for any and everything you want. You must show responsible use. The rule that I have seen is don't go over 30% of your credit utilization. If your limit is $200, do not spend more than $60 and, pay it back as soon as you can. I would shoot for even less than that. For instance, I would buy gas for $30 on Wednesday and pay it back in full on Thursday or Friday. I would do this once a week to show active use on my card. If you get a credit card, you can't just keep it in your wallet, you must be actively using it in order for it to help your credit score. Keep on being responsible with your credit card and you will be rewarded. Capital One increased my limit from $200 to $500 in a couple of months and gave me an unsecured card. I applied a couple months after that for a better card with them and was approved with a $2000 starting credit limit. That was a big deal for me when I was starting out.

I happily watched my credit score go up and up. In 2 months, it had jumped over 100 points. I learned that credit bureaus like to see a diverse credit portfolio. This just means that they like to see that you can be responsible with different types of credit. I applied for a store card and was approved. So I had a Walmart store credit card, a secured credit card, and a car note to get me started. I was responsible with all my payments and never went over the credit utilization limits I had set before. Now, I have pretty much every credit card I want in my wallet and my credit is great.

You may be thinking, "Well simple, I simply won't apply for any credit and my credit will be ok. Easy!" Nope, that won't work either. Did you know that not having credit established is just as bad as having bad credit? You will go and apply for credit one day and they will run your credit and deny you based solely on the fact that you don't have any credit. They don't know whether they can trust you or not because you don't have any historical credit data for them to go by. It's a tricky situation indeed. You have to get yourself some credit.

I have learned a couple of tricks along the way as well. You could find someone you know with good credit like your mom, spouse, grandparent, or friend. Ask them to add you to one of their credit cards as an "Authorized user" If they add you to their credit card, your credit score will jump based off their good credit history. They don't even need to get you your own card, this is good for on-paper purposes only. This helps tremendously and it's perfectly legal. I also found what is called the shopping cart trick. The shopping cart trick is used for lots of store credit cards issued by Comenity Bank. Stores like Victoria's Secret and New York and Company for example. You go to the stores' website, add items you'd like to purchase to your cart, and go to the checkout page. During the checkout process, you start entering your address and information. There is a pop up that comes up telling you

you're "Pre-approved" for the card to that store and to click yes to accept. You click yes, enter the last four digits of your social security number, and are instantly approved. You can purchase the items you wanted, or choose not to, log off the site, and wait for your card to come in the mail. The credit limits aren't huge, usually $500 or less but, it's a great way to get your foot in the door without them running your credit and doing a hard credit pull. The beauty of the shopping cart trick is they only do a "Soft pull" on your credit which doesn't negatively impact your credit. This is extremely helpful because applying for too much credit is never a good idea. Each time you apply for credit, they pull your credit report, which results in what's called a credit inquiry. Banks and lenders frown on too many inquiries in a short period of time. Also, note that every time you apply for credit, the inquiry stays on your credit report for 2 years. So, don't go applying for lots of credit cards at once, give yourself some time in between applying.

Credit bureaus judge us on our credit history, which is how long we have had credit established. They judge us on credit utilization, which is how much credit we are using. They judge us on our credit portfolios, which is how many different types of credit we have. They look at how many inquiries we have because applying for too much credit makes us look desperate and untrustworthy to them. They look at payment history as in, do you pay your bills on time? They look at negative remarks we have like collections or things that weren't paid. When things aren't paid as promised, the original company owed will often write off this debt as a loss and sell it to a collection agency. The collection company will then try to collect the funds from you. This will show up on your credit report as a negative mark or collection. See, I told you that credit charged up at 18 would come back to haunt you. Another thing to know is that negative items like collections will stay on your report for 7 years before they can be removed.

The rule of the day is to take your credit seriously. You will need it throughout life. If you ruin it, it will cost you a ton of money in interest rates and time. Start off on the right path in your journey and you will do fine. Keep your utilization low and you will be on the road to good credit. I wish I didn't have to learn this the hard way, and now you don't have to. Give yourself some credit!

21

Closing Thoughts

"Never let fear stop you from doing anything you set your mind to."
-Shaleea Venney

Life truly does feel like a maze sometimes. You have lots of obstacles to face and you're not always prepared. No doubt, you will find yourself running into the walls at times and thinking there's no way out. There is.

Find out who you are and develop a set of moral promises to yourself. You are not expected to know who you are right away, this takes time and growth. At every point in your life, try to stand for something. Know your limits, and what is not acceptable to you. Don't be afraid to go against the crowd and remove yourself from situations that make you uncomfortable.

Right now everything is a big deal and conflicts, heartaches, and trials may feel like the end of the world but don't give up. One day you'll look back and remember the things you are stressed about right now and laugh. What's a big deal now, will be nothing later.

CLOSING THOUGHTS

Stand firm on your beliefs. Never let anyone else try to tell you how or what to think. Trust your instincts. You know when something feels right or wrong in your gut. Be confident in your abilities. Humble yourself. Never think you know everything. Always be willing to learn. There is always something you don't know. Try not to be the smartest person in the room. Seek people who are smarter than you on purpose and learn everything you can from them.

Listen more than you talk. Know when to speak and when to take notes. Be kind, and genuine. Be honest. Have integrity. Say what you mean, mean what you say and be a do-er. Make things happen, don't wait for things to happen. Help others in need without expecting anything in return. Be charitable. If you can help someone, help someone.

Don't judge others based on the color of their skin, their sexual orientation, where they come from, the clothes they wear, or what you may have heard about them. If you must judge, judge people on who they are. Give people the benefit of the doubt. Judge them for how they treat you when you've had the opportunity to meet them personally. Even if they are not a good person, don't bad mouth them to others, simply acknowledge that they are not your cup of tea and sever ties. Do not take your experience with one person, out on others you meet later who remind you of them.

Forgive others. Forgiveness is one of the hardest things in the world to do when people hurt you but it is absolutely necessary for your healing. Let it go. Forgiveness doesn't mean you have to be anyone's doormat either. Forgive them to allow your heart to heal and if you choose that you no longer want anything to do with that person, it's your choice. The important thing is that you're not holding a grudge against anyone.

Have an open mind and open heart. Don't close your heart out of fear of pain or rejection. Be smart about who you share it with but, open your heart. Be passionate. Be fearless.

When you are afraid, use that adrenaline to propel you to the next level. Never let fear stop you from doing anything you set your mind to. You can achieve anything you want to if you'll do the work. Don't let the fear of failure stop you. You won't fail if you give it your all.

You are more than your bra size. You are bigger than the size of your behind. Your beauty doesn't define you. The length of your hair is not all you have to offer. You are not your body. Your heart and soul are what you make you special. Focus on building up the things about you that cannot be seen with the naked eye. Your intelligence, your faith, your confidence. Strive for substance. Please don't put all of your focus on how you look and neglect who you are. Nothing wrong with being cute, but be about something. Have dreams, goals, desires, and passions.

You will succeed. You will accomplish all that you have set out to if you never lose track of yourself. Be selfish with your time and energy while in the pursuit of your best life. It will take determination and focus but you can do it.

Life is a maze, and there are many windy roads on your journey but you will arrive at your destination. Have a little faith, girl.

God loves you and so do I!

22

Your Mistakes Are A Part of You, but Don't Define You

"Have your pity party, clean up the mess, and get back on track."
-Shaleea Venney

You are not perfect. You are going to fall, go left when you should have gone right, and make big mistakes. Let's get this understood now so that you can forgive yourself and move on. I want you to heal.

There is nothing that you could ever do that isn't beneficial to you in some way. Mistakes are the best way to be better the next time. You ever been playing a video game and get to the point in the level where you die because the character unexpectedly falls off the cliff or runs into something? It always happens when you're on a roll and so close to completing the level. What do you do? Die, start the level over, and run and jump over the part that killed you the first time.

Life is like that, without the extra lives of course. Every mistake you make, everything you do wrong, just shows you how not to make that mistake again. Failure is the best possible teacher. Sometimes we lose money, sometimes it's our pride, our hearts get broken, we sever relationships, and we fall hard. Learn your lesson. Get up, dust yourself off, and remember the speed and path you were on when you fell. Go back to the path and go for it again. This time, you'll be better equipped to avoid the fall.

You can typically get up from most of the mistakes you have made. You dropped out of school? Go back. Teenage mom? It's a bit harder now, but now you have an even stronger motivator to succeed. Love the baby and continue to strive for your greatness. Chose the wrong guy? Get out. Next time you will recognize the signs to avoid. The only thing you can't get back is time. Time will keep moving. You must not sit and wallow in your regrets for too long. Have your pity party, clean up the mess, and get back on track.

Forgive yourself. You need permission to fully forgive yourself. This is important to learn early. You will need to forgive yourself often throughout life. Accept yourself for who you are-mistakes and all. Never let anyone cast judgement on you or make you feel low for anything that you have done. If they do, remember that they are not squeaky clean either. People love to highlight your indiscretions, while burying their own. Remember that anytime someone attempts to attack your character. The only thing that matters is how you see yourself.

You can't take back your mistakes, but you don't have to take them with you where you're headed. Leave mistakes in the past where they belong. When my husband and I started off in our first apartment, we adored that little place. It was so cozy. Now that we have progressed, we have moved out of that city and on to bigger and better. When we go back to that city, we often drive past our first apartment and smile and remember those days. Imagine if we got out of the car, walked up to the door, and asked the current inhabitants if we could come inside for a tour because we once lived there. They probably wouldn't let us in. Do you know how crazy we would look for trying? We don't live there anymore. I use this story as an example. The same way we no longer live in our first apartment, is the same way you can't live in the past. Move on. You must move on. Your past should be a point of reference to show you how far you've come. Look back at it if you need to from time to time and keep going. You're off to bigger and better, the past will only weigh your future down. Plus, there won't be any room for extra baggage in the beautiful future you're on the road to.

Remember the pain, failure, and setbacks. Use them on your journey ahead as a compass. Those lessons will come in handy one day. You're wiser because of them. Zero regrets.

23

Might I Suggest You See The World?

"You can learn lots of things about yourself when you get outside of your comfort zone."
-Shaleea Venney

If the opportunity presents itself for you to get out and travel, don't hesitate. Get your passport as soon as you can. Passports give you the freedom to roam this planet as you please. Take planes, boats, trains, and automobiles as far as they may take you. Wake up in as many new locations as you possibly can. Smell the air. Watch the sun set. Make friends from different cultures, and backgrounds. Get lost on purpose. The world is beautifully and wonderfully made to be explored and admired.

You can learn lots of things about yourself when you get outside of your comfort zone. Nothing like an unfamiliar location to bring out your inner adventurer. You might be amazed at how resourceful you can be when you don't speak a language but have a need arise. You will never forget the way the food tastes in one place, and how they drive in another. How the things that one country deems as normal, are completely unacceptable and rude in another. It's so much fun and it will make you grow as a person.

It is my hope that you create beautiful memories that you can always cherish. Some of your best times will be had in the most unexpected places. Don't always go to places that everyone else wants to go to. Explore unique and different places that may not be on everyone's radar. Places that you never thought you'd go. These are the places that surprise you the most. Be well traveled. Traveling will expand your mind, give you a different perspective, encourage growth and self-reflection, and make you a stronger and more confident person to name a few things.

If you can take some time off when you graduate high school, go. If you can go on summer vacations, do it. Visit places that take your breath away and awaken your soul. Create what I call a "Gotta Go list". Compile a list of all the places you dream of going to and start crossing them off as you get to them. Check each place you see off the list as you visit them and add more to the list along the way. This is the same thing as what some people call a bucket list but I don't believe that you should wait till you get older to travel. Quite the contrary, go while you're young and active enough to hike the trails, walk many miles, and see many moons. Live your life to the fullest while you can.

When you find love, travel with your spouse. Share firsts with each other. Go someplace you've never been together. Kiss under international skies. Fall in love with each other again in different places. Try different foods. Practice speaking the native language. Hang with the locals. Venture off the tourist paths- within safe reason of course. Share as many experiences with each other while traveling as possible. Nothing like seeing the world together to strengthen your bond.

Travel as much as you can before you have children. Once you grow up and have responsibilities like having children, it's harder and harder to travel. Plus, traveling is much different and more expensive when you have children in tow. You are restricted to places you can see, and things you can do when you have children. Introduce them to travel too but, make plans to go on at least one trip a year without them. You need to get out with your husband and reconnect someplace beautiful just the two of you. This will do wonders for your relationship.

Work and or study abroad. Teach English as a second language. Volunteer in an impoverished part of the world. Do missionary work. You can combine your love for traveling with your love for helping others in need. It can be rewarding in many ways.

I hope your thirst for adventure never ends. Go as often and as far as you can. I hope you do a safari in Africa, visit the pyramids in Egypt, snorkel on beautiful islands, see the Middle East, Asia, backpack across Europe, and visit South America. I hope you get away. Traveling is one of the best things you could ever do for yourself. It costs to travel but, you will create priceless memories and experiences that will last a lifetime. Get out there and explore. It will change your life.

24

I'm A Big Girl Now

"Class has only gone out of style to the people who don't have any."
-Shaleea Venney

So you're grown now? You made it to your big 18th birthday. Perhaps you're legal age-21. Nobody can tell you anything, cause you already know. You make your own decisions. You do what feels right to you and are completely unapologetic about it. Kudos to you. But can we talk candidly between you and I while there's no one around?

There are many "Grown women" who are secretly drowning in little girl issues on the inside. "Grown women" who exude confidence and appear to have it all together but, are crying themselves to sleep at night. I've seen countless "Grown women" who simply got older in a numbers sense but, didn't mature in the least. Be honest, I won't tell anyone. What is the little girl living inside of you trying to tell you? What has she carried into your adulthood that still haunts you because you haven't acknowledged it yet? Don't deny it. If you could speak to the little girl living inside of you, what would you say to her? What would she say to you?

The thing about regret is that regret is like a lingering odor following you around. It won't go away until you address it. Other people can smell it on you because of your actions or attitude but they're not quite sure what that smell is. They don't know where the smell is coming from, but you do. The stench of your disappointment is strong, and it's affecting your overall health and wellness. It's affecting your relationships, and your self esteem. It's time to make a change. I know you're a big girl now, but the only way to actually be a big girl is to look at your issues head on and address them. Only then, can you change.

Perhaps you were molested, maybe you missed the love of your father, it's possible you never got that degree you wanted to, or dropped out of high school. You might regret becoming a teen mother, or that you gained a lot more weight than you would've liked to. You might not have very high self esteem or you may be battling depression. Maybe you're alone, or even worse, are surrounded by people who don't even know you-that's real loneliness. Figure out what it is that you're holding on to cause that's the only way you can put it down.

Being "Grown" doesn't mean you're supposed to have all the answers. Don't be afraid to seek the counsel of your elders and other women who have been there. The most important thing is who you are listening to. Watch out for people with negative spirits and people who are constantly going through things. Those energies can jump onto you and if you are not careful, you will unintentionally become just like those people. Be very careful taking advice from blind people. By blind, I mean people who have no vision. Be very careful when taking advice from bitter people, or people who are generally not on the same page as you. Even if they are on the same page as where you are now, you need people who can speak to where you are headed. Stagnant people will never be able to educate you on the flow of life.

Don't allow any man to treat you or talk to you like you don't matter.

Don't make excuses for him or stay with him out of loyalty, break free from him so that you can have a chance to be loved the way you deserve. Life is too short. Don't settle for any man out of fear that you'll be alone. It is better to be alone than to be with someone who doesn't mean you any well, cause a relationship like that makes you feel alone anyway. When you are ready to find a man, look for someone with substance and good character. Don't be the girl who gets with the guy with 8 baby mothers thinking you can change him, you'll be baby mother number nine. 8 baby mothers says a ton about his character and is a red flag, have some sense sis. This is just an example of course but you get the point. Same thing applies to the dope dealer, and the thug. Entertaining these type of men, comes with a lot of drama and is quite honestly dangerous due to the lifestyles they lead. Not saying that any of these guys are bad people, they're just lost and it's easy to get lost with them. It's quite difficult for a man to give you stability and a family when his lifestyle isn't conducive to peace. Quit overlooking nice guys for trap dudes, and dudes hanging on the block. Find a guy with some maturity who wants more out of life.

Single mothers, you are the super heroes of the world. You give so much to make sure every need is taken care of. You often neglect yourself and rarely ever get a thank you. Your hard work is not in vain. Please focus on your children and being the best woman and mother possible for them. If your baby's father is a deadbeat, don't teach your children this by talking about him to them. Your children need to make their own decisions about who their fathers are and they will eventually see for themselves. Don't try to teach them to hate him if you do. Never use your children to hurt their fathers. If your relationship didn't end well, he is still just as much their father as you are their mother. Never use children as a pawn. It's disgusting and unfair to the children and they lose in the end. If he wants to be a father, put on your big girl panties, and let him- in peace and without all the extra comments and remarks. Never try to hurt a man by filing child support documents against him if he didn't deserve it. I am all for having a man take care of his responsibility, but if he is contributing financially, don't go running down to the courthouse because you're bitter because he has someone new or you're mad at him and want to get back at him. You have no right to tell him he can't move on. Move on. Try to work out the financial aspect of child care one on one without involving the courts if possible. If you can't work it out and do file for child support, remember one thing: Child support is for the child, not for you. The same way you want him to get a job, is the same way you should have one too. Get your own hair and nails done and buy your children what they need with the allocated funds. No man should need to take care of a grown woman. Get your own. Period.

Hold yourself to a higher standard ladies. No grown woman should *want* to be a side chick. Your dream man will not come perfectly packaged, fully assembled, with a wife. If he is married leave him alone period. A man will always do what we as women allow them to. Yes it is true that he is the one who took the vows to his wife but where are the vows you made to yourself? You shouldn't be anyone's piece of tail. The reality is, he's probably not going to leave his wife, no matter what he tells you. Why would he? He already has both of you. If by some chance he does leave his wife, are you going to be happy? What sort of prize do you think you've won? Congratulations! You get a cheater! If he cheated with you, do you honestly think he won't cheat on you. Your lady parts are not so good that he won't cheat on you. You are not that special. His cheating with you most likely had nothing to do with his wife and they probably still have great sex. Look at women like Halle Berry or Beyonce and ask yourself how they could be cheated on as beautiful as they are. It's not about them! It's a character trait in the men. They are just disloyal.

I feel like some of you are reading this thinking, "So what! I am only in it for the sex and his wife can have him. I don't even want to be in a relationship" Girl Bye!!! Please stop, take a look in the mirror and get some self esteem with a side of self worth! If you feel that sex is just sex, then have it with one of the many single men out there. Sex is just sex, until you end up pregnant by that married man. Sex is just sex until you catch feelings for that married man who is emotionally unavailable to you. Get it together sis! You could have a whole man to yourself without all the messiness. If you can't get it together for any other reason, Karma! Karma is real dear. You will reap what you sow one day. I'd hate for you to fall in love with some man, marry him, and think all is well and that you're happy. What if one day your husband runs into a woman like you and destroys your heart like you did that man's wife? Think about it. I am married so of course my outlook is that of the wife. But if I became suddenly single tomorrow, I would never be the side chick-knowingly. I simply know what I deserve and what I am worth and will not be anyone's second choice. Focus on self love as you are coming into your own. You need to learn to like yourself now and hold onto those feelings as you continue to get older. I promise you it's not always easy to do but if you master this feeling for yourself, it will greatly change the way you see yourself and what you tolerate from others.

I do not expect every one of you to be Michelle Obama types, but I do expect for you to not be afraid to try to be *something*. This day and age means I am grown, my body is grown, and I can show it off. There's a time and place for that. You don't have to post a million nude pictures on social media to get likes. Every picture you take doesn't have to show off your behind. What are you trying to prove to yourself or to the world? Do you need people to tell you you're attractive, or that your body is nice? Do you need men to jump in your DMs to boost your self esteem? You don't have to give away everything you have on social media. I might be a prude or old school but, I don't feel like everyone should be able to see me naked. That's reserved for a select person, and a level of intimacy that you don't get online. A guy should be able to talk to you without having already seen you naked. I know, this is tough because you need the attention but doing this attracts the wrong attention and anyone with any substance won't take you seriously. Your body is special and so are you, don't give it to everyone for free on social media. Class has only gone out of style to the people who don't have any.

25

Give Thanks!

"There will always be consequences, good or bad."
-Shaleea Venney

When you are trying to come to a decision about anything that concerns you, use my acronym before you do. Always give THANKS: Think about what you're planning to do and how it will benefit you. Question the consequences to your actions. There will always be consequences, good or bad. Never make a rushed decision because you make mistakes when you rush, don't be anxious for anything. Pray about it. Ask God for His guidance and Seek his advice. Don't just pray about it, wait to hear from God. What is God telling you to do? Take your time. Sometimes one decision can change your entire life within a matter of minutes and you will never be able to get a do-over. Give T.H.A.N.K.S. before deciding what your next step should be.

Think about what you are about to do.

How will it benefit you?

Ask yourself what the consequences are.

Never make a rushed decision or be anxious about anything.

Kneel down and pray about it.

Seek God's guidance. Wait to hear from God before moving forward

About the Author

Shaleea Venney is an Author, Speaker, Blogger, and host of the Girl Which Way?! Podcast. She is a Wife, Mother of 2, Licensed Nurse, and a little girl who lost her way.

As the Founder and President of the Non-Profit Organization Venney Girl Inc. Shaleea is an advocate for young women and teen moms everywhere and has a passion for helping young women be their best selves and thrive. She is a firm believer that where you start, has no bearing on how you finish, and that all young women can succeed when they are provided with the proper tools. If you would like to learn more about Shaleea and or connect with her further, please visit ShaleeaVenney.com

www.ingramcontent.com/pod-product-compliance
Lightning Source LLC
Chambersburg PA
CBHW050303010526
44108CB00040B/2166